Butterflies
of the British Isles

Jeremy Thomas

illustrated by
Gordon Riley and Ken Oliver

NEWNES

COUNTRY LIFE BOOKS

595.789

38239

B0005864

ACKNOWLEDGEMENTS

MS Warren and KJ Willmott have been characteristically generous in loaning photographs of young stages in their natural settings, and have made invaluable suggestions and corrections to the text, as have N Lear and my patient editor Trevor Dolby. Responsibility for any errors, however, is my own. I have also been very fortunate in the help and encouragement given by my wife Sarah, to whom this book is dedicated. Finally, I owe a special debt to many predecessors, notably FW Frohawk, EB Ford, Edmund Sandars and, more recently, Margaret Brooks, for the inspiration and knowledge they have imparted.

The publishers would like to make special acknowledgement to Mr David Clark for generously allowing the use of 20 of his 30 transparencies in this book, free of charge, in recognition of the work done by the RSNC for the conservation of butterflies in Britain. Also Peter Cribb for the loan of specimens for artist's reference.

BUTTERFLIES AND THE LAW

It is illegal to catch or collect any stage of these butterflies in Britain without a licence from the Nature Conservancy Council:

> Heath Fritillary
> Chequered Skipper
> Swallowtail
> Large Blue

It is not illegal to possess either set specimens or livestock of these species that were originally caught before the passing of the Wildlife and Countryside Act in 1981.

Published by Country Life Books
an imprint of Newnes Books
a Division of the Hamlyn Publishing Group Limited,
Bridge House, 69 London Road, Twickenham,
Middlesex, England, and distributed for them by
The Hamlyn Publishing Group Limited,
Rushden, Northants, England.

Text © Jeremy Thomas 1986
Illustrations © pages 5 (top), 26-39, 57-58 Stan Morse, Midsummer Books with the exception of Lulworth Skipper (♂), Silver-spotted Skipper (underwing), Clouded Yellow (*helice*), Brimstone (♀ upperside), Green-veined White (summer ♀), N. Brown Argus, Common Blue (♀), Purple Emperor (♀), High Brown Fritillary, Silver-washed Fritillary (*valezina*), Large Heath (*scotica*), and pages 46-155 © Country Life Books, a Division of the Hamlyn Publishing Group Limited 1986.

First published 1986
ISBN 0 600 351 904 (softback)
ISBN 0 600 550 648 (hardback)
Printed in Italy

Contents

INTRODUCTION

This guide has been written for the growing number of field naturalists who wish to discover and identify the wild butterflies of Britain. Wherever possible, I have avoided the use of scientific jargon, in the hope that beginners and children will not be overawed by what is really rather an easy subject to master. On the other hand, I have tried to interest the more expert naturalist by including as much new information as possible about the biology and distribution of our butterflies.

The book has three main sections. The first contains a brief account of the structure and life cycle of a butterfly, and describes how different species live in different habitats. Next is a sixteen-page identification guide, where all except the rarest vagrants are illustrated side by side, with notes on how to distinguish between them. This leads into the main part of the book: a detailed account of the natural history of each species, including illustrations of the whole life cycle and as much other information as space permits. The young stages have been especially drawn to show how they appear in their natural surroundings; caterpillars and chrysalises are life size, but the eggs are enlarged about seven times.

Every resident species in Britain and all the regular immigrants from abroad are included in the main sections, a total of 58 species. Rare vagrants, that one might encounter once in a lifetime, are relegated to the final pages, alongside brief descriptions of the Large Blue and Large Copper.

BUTTERFLY OR MOTH?

Butterflies and moths form a large group of related insects, the *Lepidoptera*, which differ from all other insects in having wings that are covered with minute, overlapping scales. Another unique feature is the adult's proboscis: a long tube for a mouth, which is normally kept coiled beneath the head but can be extended like a straw to drink liquids. About 2400 species of *Lepidoptera* are regularly found in Britain, but only 58 of these are butterflies; the rest are moths. With practice, it is easy to distinguish between the two groups, although there are few hard and fast rules.

All butterflies fly during the day and most are brightly coloured; moths tend to be nocturnal and are often rather drab. British butterflies have quite thin bodies and, with one exception, shut their wings together above the body when they rest. Many moths are fat and furry, and settle in various postures, often with the wings draped round the body. There are, nevertheless, several coloured day-flying moths. The surest way to distinguish between these and butterflies is to examine the antennae (feelers): those of butterflies are slender and always end in a swollen tip or club; only Burnet moths (opposite) have anything approaching clubbed antennae – the rest come in various shapes ranging from single strands to intricate feathers.

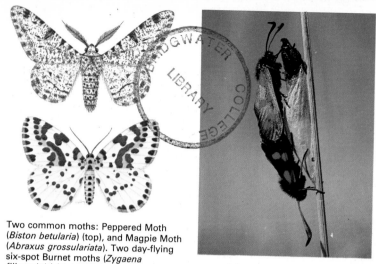

Two common moths: Peppered Moth (*Biston betularia*) (top), and Magpie Moth (*Abraxus grossulariata*). Two day-flying six-spot Burnet moths (*Zygaena filipendula*) (right). Note the wings folded around the furry body, and curved, tapering, club-shaped antennae.

THE LIFE CYCLE AND STRUCTURE OF A BUTTERFLY

Every butterfly goes through four very different stages during its life. It starts as an *egg* which hatches to produce a minute *caterpillar*. This feeds and grows enormously before changing into a *chrysalis*, from which the final stage, the *adult* butterfly, later emerges. Before dying, female adults lay many eggs to begin a new generation of butterflies. Some species take a whole year to complete this cycle, others fit in two, three, or even four generations between spring and autumn, but as winter approaches, all butterflies must hibernate or die. Hibernation can occur in any stage of the life cycle, but the stage used is always constant for a particular species.

(Illustration *not* to scale)

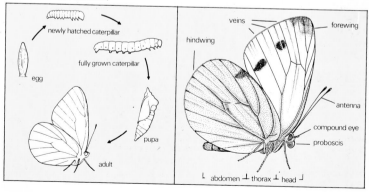

The adult

The adult's body is divided into three distinct sections: head, thorax and abdomen. The head has two eyes, two antennae used for smelling and balance, and an extendable proboscis which it uses for drinking nectar and other liquids.

The thorax is the power box that operates three pairs of legs (although the front pair is stunted in some species) and two pairs of wings. Each wing is a double layer of thin transparent membrane, stretched between rigid veins through which blood flows. Microscopic scales cover the wings, arranged rather like tiles on a roof. Many are pigmented and others reflect or refract the light, producing iridescent colours.

The wings have many uses in addition to flight. The pattern of the underwing may camouflage the adult, whilst false eyespots and tails trick enemies into believing that the vulnerable head is elsewhere. The bright colours often attract the opposite sex, and males have special scent scales on the upper forewings that produce aphrodisiacs. In addition, dark scales along the veins of many species absorb the sun's warmth and heat the blood, whereas the underwings are often shiny, allowing overheated adults to cool down by reflecting the sun.

The abdomen contains the adult's reproductive organs. After an often elaborate courtship, butterflies mate back to back (see page 87) and the female later lays eggs through the tip of her abdomen (see page 59).

The main activities of an adult's life are to mate and, in the case of a female, to lay as many eggs as possible in the most suitable places for their survival. Adults that hibernate also need to build up large reserves of food by drinking nectar, and before they can do anything, all adults must warm their bodies to a remarkably high temperature — around 32° to 35°C. This they do by altering the area of wing surface exposed to the sun.

The egg, caterpillar and chrysalis

Butterfly eggs are of various shapes and sizes, as can be seen in the accounts of individual species. In detail, each consists of a hard outer shell which is particularly robust in those species that hibernate in this stage. At the top of the egg is a small depression, the micropyle, where the shell is thin, allowing oxygen to enter. Young eggs contain a mass of nutritious fluid and a microscopic embryo which soon absorbs the fluid and grows into a little caterpillar. This nibbles its way out, often eating the whole eggshell.

The caterpillar is the main feeding stage in the life cycle and the only one that grows. It possesses a pair of powerful jaws that are well able to chew plant leaves or flowers, in contrast to the adult which can feed only on liquids. There is a long body, bearing six true legs behind the head, four pairs of suckers (prolegs) further back, and another (the clasper) at the end. A caterpillar's skin is thin and flexible, but as the body grows, it can eventually stretch no further and is shed. By then, a new larger skin has already developed beneath the old one, often rather different in shape and colour. The number of moults in a caterpillar's life varies from 3 to 6, depending on the species. When full grown, the skin is shed for the last time, to reveal a chrysalis underneath.

This Silver-studded Blue's egg (right) is the size of a pin-head. The Purple Emperor caterpillar (top) is camouflaged to look like a Sallow leaf. The chrysalis of the Chalkhill Blue (bottom) bears the impression of the adult inside.

The chrysalis is the transitional stage when the caterpillar's body tissues are converted into an adult butterfly. While the hard outer case appears immobile, almost all the contents inside are being reassembled from a sort of living soup. When fully formed, the adult breaks open the chrysalis case and emerges. At first the wings are small soft pads. They are blown up by pumping blood into the veins, and set hard after an hour or two.

COLONIES AND NUMBERS

Most British butterflies live in discrete colonies which breed in the same small areas, or close by, year after year. A typical colony fluctuates considerably in size, ranging from under fifty adults in a poor season to a few hundred in a good one. Some sites contain much larger populations of tens or even hundreds of thousands, but these are most unusual.

In the colony, there are generally equal numbers of males and females, although it often looks as if males predominate because the females tend to be inconspicuous. Every female present has the potential to lay several hundred eggs. In practice, fifty eggs per female is a good average, for many die before laying their full capacity. This nevertheless gives the colony an enormous potential to increase if conditions are favourable, for only two offspring need survive – to produce one male and one female – if the colony is to remain stable.

From the moment the eggs are laid it is a race against death. Unless they hibernate, typical eggs hatch after seven to ten days, by which time perhaps one in twenty will have been killed by disease, predators, or parasitic wasp larvae that are so tiny that up to twenty can develop inside a single pinhead-sized egg. Caterpillars are much more vulnerable, being killed mainly by other insects and spiders when small and by birds, shrews and mice as they grow larger. Many caterpillars are beautifully

7

camouflaged to escape these predators; others are poisonous or have sharp spines, and generally live in large groups which enhances this deterrent and, incidentally, makes them very easy for the naturalist to find. Unfortunately, they are equally conspicuous to parasitic wasps and flies, that are not deterred by these defences and which kill vast numbers of gregarious caterpillars. Blues have a more subtle form of protection that is highly effective against predators and parasites. Sweet liquids from a gland and pores, ooze over their bodies and attract ants which attend them day and night, and fiercely repel any enemies.

Up to two thirds of the caterpillars in a typical colony are killed, but this still leaves an average of about fifteen, from each mother that laid the original eggs, to form chrysalises. Unfortunately, the chrysalis is even more prone to attack; indeed four-fifths or more of the population may be killed during this period. Birds and small mammals are again the chief culprits, and again many extraordinary forms of camouflage have evolved to combat them. Some chrysalises even live inside ant nests.

In addition to avoiding their enemies, caterpillars have to feed. Most species eat only one or a few closely related types of wild plant, and often, only a certain part of the plant, for example the flowers or young leaf-tips, is palatable. Yet another requirement of some species is that they need to live in unusually warm places if they are to survive for, being cold-blooded, they take longer to develop in cool spots and this gives their enemies more time to find them. The twin needs of survival and special foodplants restrict the caterpillars of each species to living in a small and specialised part of its environment, be it in a wood, grassland or heathland.

Adult female butterflies take great care to lay eggs in the exact places where they are most likely to survive. Experienced naturalists know exactly where to look for different species, and can often find the young stages with remarkable ease.

The Adonis Blue caterpillar eats low-growing Horseshoe Vetch leaves. The red ant is milking its posterior gland for sweet secretions.

Adult movements and migrations

About three-quarters of the British species live in close-knit colonies, breeding in small discrete areas from which the adults very rarely stray. The other quarter are much more mobile and fly freely through the countryside, laying eggs wherever suitable conditions are encountered. These species include several of our most familiar butterflies, for example the Small Tortoiseshell and Brimstone. Some species also mix with continental populations, for example Large and Small Whites often cross the Channel, in both directions.

There are a few butterflies that regularly migrate to Britain. The Red Admiral, Painted Lady and Clouded Yellow cannot survive a British winter, except in insignificant numbers, but permanent populations breed round the Mediterranean and in North Africa. All produce vast swarms that fly north each spring to breed throughout Europe during the summer months. Some always reach southern England, and the Red Admiral is generally common. The Clouded Yellow is more sporadic, but in freak 'Clouded Yellow Years' large numbers arrive and are a common sight throughout the British Isles. There is some evidence that migratory butterflies return south in autumn, but it is thought that most perish. In addition to the regular migrants, there are several other species that reach Britain very rarely (see pages 157-158).

DISTRIBUTION AND HABITATS

Most mobile species of butterfly may be encountered almost anywhere within the British Isles, but many sedentary species have limited ranges and very patchy distributions within their ranges. This is due to the reluctance of the adults to leave their breeding grounds. Suitable sites, and hence colonies, may be few and far between, perhaps because the caterpillar's foodplant grows only on particular soils, or because it can survive only on hot places in the south. There is a noticeable fall in the number of species as one travels north, and islands also tend to have fewer butterflies.

WOODLAND

Woods differ enormously in the number of butterflies they contain. The richest examples have 35-40 different species, yet many are depressing places with no more than a few of the commonest butterflies. Some of these differences reflect geology and geography. Regional differences are small, however, when compared with the high degree of local variation that often occurs between woods in the same neighbourhood. The extent to which a wood fulfils the potential for its region depends, very largely, on its internal structure and on how it has been managed.

All woods, even the shadiest, attract up to twelve mobile species which arrive periodically to feed on flowers. Three – the Clouded Yellow, Large and Small Whites – never breed there, but the rest lay eggs if their foodplants are encountered, before moving on. These latter butterflies include the Brimstone, Comma, Peacock and Holly Blue.

The other thirty species that can be found in woods are more sedentary and will be present only if the site contains enough of the caterpillar's foodplant, growing under the right conditions, to support a whole colony year after year.

The precise places used for breeding are described under the accounts of individual species, and are summarised in the illustration opposite. Rather surprisingly, the caterpillars of only four butterflies feed on trees, while another six species eat different kinds of shrubs and climbers. In contrast, no fewer than 33 butterflies breed on various low-growing plants on the forest floor. These ground-living butterflies can roughly be divided into two groups: those that need fresh clearings where their foodplants briefly flourish before being shaded out again, and those that breed in rides, glades, and wood edges. The first group includes several characteristic woodland butterflies, notably those Fritillaries that depend on a flush of violets for breeding. In contrast, rides, glades and edges are no more than sheltered strips of permanent grassland, and they support some typically grassland butterflies, for example the Browns and golden Skippers. This distinction is imprecise for a few species: Common Blue, Wood White, Small Copper, Grizzled and Dingy Skipper can live in rides, but all do better in regenerating clearings.

In recent years, modern methods of forestry have transformed the structure of many woods and this, in turn, has caused dramatic changes in the status of several woodland butterflies. Clearings, nowadays, tend to be few and far between, and the floors of most woods are very much shadier than in the past, when practices such as coppicing created a constant supply of fresh openings. This has had a catastrophic effect on Fritillaries and other sun-loving butterflies that need fresh ground. On the other hand, modern rides are often kept wide for large vehicles, and many so-called 'grassland' butterflies still flourish in woods that have lost their 'woodland' species. Most of the butterflies that breed on shrubs are holding their own in modern woods, but those that need deciduous trees have been greatly harmed by the switch to conifers, and Dutch Elm disease has caused serious declines in the White-letter Hairstreak. On the credit side, the Speckled Wood and White Admiral prefer slightly shaded conditions, and these beautiful butterflies have actually been spreading in British woods.

Butterfly watching in woods

It follows from the above that the finest woods for butterflies are large forest complexes that have a history of recent clearings, a considerable diversity of structure, and many sunny areas. On the whole, deciduous woods are much better than conifers, although young plantations on ancient sites may briefly support an abundance of rare species.

Egglaying females tend to be inconspicuous, and the best places to watch butterflies are not necessarily where breeding occurs. Most species congregate in sunny rides and glades where, in season, scores of Browns, Skippers, Nymphalids and perhaps Fritillaries jostle for nectar. Some have favourite flowers: the short-tongued Gatekeeper prefers Ragwort or Fleabane whereas Brimstone and Peacock can reach down the long tubes of Teasels. Everything likes Bramble, and it is much easier to wait by a sunny patch and let the butterflies come to you. At other times of the day or year, the same species that are seen on flowers will be more interested in finding mates, and this takes them into different parts of the wood. The males of most species either patrol the rides or perch in wait for females, and you will soon discover the characteristic places used by each. In slightly shaded areas, look for the male Speckled Wood as he perches in a sunbeam or indulges in a dancing flight there.

Much will be missed if butterfly watching is confined to eyelevel. Several species live mainly on the canopy, and binoculars are essential to see these properly. Stand in a glade where the bushy treetops are visible, and perhaps you will see a Hairstreak looping briefly above the canopy in a rapid tumbling flight. Sometimes, they can be dislodged by tapping the lowest boughs, but many more are seen if you climb a tall tree and gaze down over the treetops. There, in the richest woods, Meadow Browns, Gatekeepers, Speckled Woods, White Admirals and Large Fritillaries will also be seen crawling over the uppermost leaves, drinking the sweet honeydew secreted by aphids. Most spectacular of all, although very scarce, is the master tree of a Purple Emperor colony. The males congregate from wide areas onto a prominent tree and perch on particular twigs, frequently ascending to battle in violent clashing flights.

The eggs and caterpillars of many woodland butterflies are even easier to find than the adult. They have the benefit of being visible in the evening, in dull as well as in fine weather, and extend the field season round the whole year. Details and practical hints on how to find each species are given in its individual account.

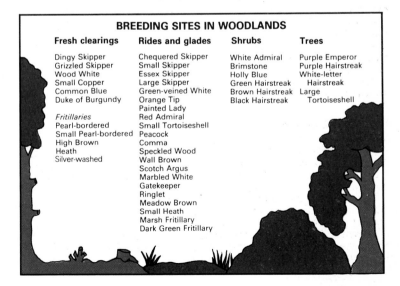

BREEDING SITES IN WOODLANDS

Fresh clearings	Rides and glades	Shrubs	Trees
Dingy Skipper	Chequered Skipper	White Admiral	Purple Emperor
Grizzled Skipper	Small Skipper	Brimstone	Purple Hairstreak
Wood White	Essex Skipper	Holly Blue	White-letter
Small Copper	Large Skipper	Green Hairstreak	Hairstreak
Common Blue	Green-veined White	Brown Hairstreak	Large
Duke of Burgundy	Orange Tip	Black Hairstreak	Tortoiseshell
	Painted Lady		
Fritillaries	Red Admiral		
Pearl-bordered	Small Tortoiseshell		
Small Pearl-bordered	Peacock		
High Brown	Comma		
Heath	Speckled Wood		
Silver-washed	Wall Brown		
	Scotch Argus		
	Marbled White		
	Gatekeeper		
	Ringlet		
	Meadow Brown		
	Small Heath		
	Marsh Fritillary		
	Dark Green Fritillary		

Woodland Butterflies

Purple Hairstreak

male

female

Holly Blue

Purple Emperor

female
underwing

male

The Purple Hairstreak and Purple Emperor are virtually confined to woodland, and are best watched through binoculars for they rarely descend to ground level. They breed, respectively, in Oaks and Sallows, and drink aphid honeydew, which often coats the treetops.

The White Admiral is a common sight along rides in large southern woods. It prefers slightly shady areas, where the caterpillar's foodplant, honeysuckle, grows as strands in dappled light. Shrubs bordering sunny rides and wood edges attract egglaying Holly Blues and Brimstones. The former uses the flowers and fruit of several bushes, whilst the latter breeds on the leaves of Buckthorns.

Freshly cut coppice, and other clearings, create a flush of violets which are the food of several Fritillaries. Look for the Pearl-bordered Fritillary in the most recent and sunniest openings in late May and for the magnificent Silver-washed Fritillary in July in slightly shadier clearings, where some taller trees remain.

White Admiral

Brimstone

male

female

male

female

Speckled Wood

male

Silver-washed Fritillary

Pearl-bordered Fritillary

Ringlet

Grassy areas in woods, such as rides and glades, support a different range of butterflies from the recent clearings. These are the breeding grounds of several Skippers and Browns, which may be equally common in open grassland. However, the Speckled Wood and Ringlet are especially characteristic of woods. The former breeds along the semi-shaded edges whilst the Ringlet needs sunnier spaces, that are damp and overgrown with tall grass.

GRASSLAND

Grasslands of one type or another cover most of the British Isles and are the main breeding grounds for the majority of our species. Unfortunately, a high proportion of fields in the lowlands has been ruined for butterflies by agricultural improvement. This eliminates all the native plants on which caterpillars depend. At best, only Clouded Yellows can breed there, using sown Clovers.

Entomologists soon learn to concentrate on 'natural' grassland that has never been sprayed or reseeded. Vast acreages still survive in northern uplands and moors (pages 18-19); but in the south, breeding sites have largely been reduced to verges, woodland rides, the coastline, Army Ranges, and steep hillsides. The variety of butterflies to be found there varies with the geology, local climate, topography and soil. Richest of all grasslands are the southfacing slopes of chalk and limestone hills. This is due partly to their calcareous soils, which support a range of foodplants that are rare or absent elsewhere and partly to their warm aspects which provide rare breeding sites for species like the Adonis Blue which are better adapted to the hot climate of central Europe.

Management also has a crucial influence on the range of butterflies that is present. Fields soon revert to coarse grass and scrub if not periodically mown or grazed. There is a succession of species that flourish in swards of different heights and densities.

Very few butterflies breed in arid sun-baked turf that is really short or sparse, but for the Adonis Blue, Silver-spotted Skipper and some other

Ant hills and an abundance of wild flowers are sure signs that this unimproved grassland is a rich breeding place for butterflies.

rarities, this is essential. A wide range of Blues and other typical downland species inhabit grassland that is only slightly taller. All are gradually shaded out, together with their foodplants, once the turf exceeds eight cm or so in height. Then other species proliferate: most Browns flourish in medium to tall grassland, and they in turn are replaced by several Skippers in very overgrown swards that are dominated by tussocks of coarse grasses.

The richest grasslands are those that have a patchwork of grass heights, with short thin-soiled slopes interspersed between medium and tall areas. This occurs naturally on eroding undercliffs, and often in abandoned quarries and pits. It has also been created, with breathtaking success, by selective grazing on some nature reserves. Such diversity is unusual, however, in most unimproved grassland, which is either farmed or abandoned. In the past, short open swards predominated due to intensive rabbit grazing. After myxomatosis in the 1950s, the sward grew to the opposite extreme. Countless colonies of Blues and other 'short grass' species disappeared, but Browns and some Skippers became abundant. Very recently, there has been a partial return of rabbits, and a rich mixture of short and taller turf has been recreated on many sites.

Butterfly watching in grassland

Grassland is best explored in warm still weather, for most butterflies are grounded on windy days. The males of several species gather towards the bases of hills and in sheltered hollows, where they await females. All behave rather differently there: certain Blues and Browns will be found settled on the ground, others patrol backwards and forwards. The Green Hairstreak, Duke of Burgundy and Large Skipper establish individual perching posts on prominent branches of shrubs, or tall tussocks. Any male is easy to approach and photograph on his perching post. He remains in position for hours, invariably returning to the same twig or leaf when disturbed.

In early evening, male and female Blues are to be found roosting in groups on tall grass clumps, again usually in sheltered hollows or along the bases of hills. There may be large numbers on each clump, sometimes consisting of several species, more often each in its own group. Roosts are easy to find by crouching and scanning the grassheads at eye level. It is well worth watching one in the morning when it is first exposed to full sunshine. For a few minutes, every adult basks with its wings wide open before dispersing. Early morning and late afternoon are the best times to photograph both Blues and Browns; during the heat of the day, most sit with their wings half or completely closed, and Browns, in particular, are hard to approach.

The young stages can also be found once one has learnt the plants and situations chosen for egglaying. Start with easy species such as the eggs of Duke of Burgundy, Small Copper and most Blues. Blue caterpillars are best discovered by scanning the foodplant for an excited group of ants, then searching beneath for a beautifully camouflaged caterpillar. Brown caterpillars hide deep in grassclumps by day, but ascend to eat the tender leaf tips after dark. They can easily be spotted by torchlight. Different grasses, growing in particular places, will yield different species; all are easy to rear, as are Blue caterpillars with or without ants.

Chalk Downland Butterflies

female

Chalkhill Blue

male

caterpillar

Common Blue

male

male

female

Adonis Blue

male

Small Blue

Blue butterflies are among the chief delights of southern chalk and limestone hills. Five grassland species may be present on the best sites, as well as the Holly Blue if shrubs or trees are present. The Brown Argus is the first to emerge, and by late May Common, Adonis and Small Blues are also well out, together with their close relatives, the Small Copper and Green Hairstreak. These six Lycaenids last well into June. There is then a lull before the first Chalkhill Blues emerge. August provides another magnificent display with the Chalkhills, then at their peak, joined by second broods of Brown Argus, Common and Adonis Blues. There may be tens of thousands of Blues flying together on exceptional sites.

Most other characteristic grassland butterflies belong to the Skipper and Brown families. Dingy Skipper, Small Heath and Wall emerge in May followed by further broods of the last two species in August and September. However, the majority of Browns and Skippers fly in July and August, amply compensating for the temporary lack of Blues. Typical examples are Meadow Brown, Marbled White, and the Large and Small Skipper.

Green Hairstreak

Dingy Skipper

Meadow Brown
male

Small Heath

female

Brown Argus

mating
Marbled Whites

Small Skipper

Large Skipper
caterpillar

Large Skipper

Wall Brown

Small Copper

HEATHS, MOORS, BOGS AND MOUNTAINS

These wild treeless habitats support a small but distinctive range of butterflies, including several species that are rare or absent elsewhere.

Heaths are open areas in lowland Britain, where ancient forest clearances have left sandy exposures too poor to develop into true grassland. Most heaths are dominated by heathers, and support a limited number of low-growing plants, with few grasses except in the wetter areas. In late summer Small Tortoiseshell, Painted Lady, and other Vanessids are attracted to the flowering heather, but seldom breed there. Characteristic breeding species include Small Heath, Gatekeeper, Common Blue, Small Copper and Green Hairstreak, but all are commonest where the land has been disturbed and, to some extent, enriched. There are, however, two butterflies that are especially characteristic of pure heathland: Grayling and Silver-studded Blue. Graylings live in the driest spots where there are patches of exposed sand and sparse tufts of fine grasses on which the caterpillars feed. Although now very rare elsewhere (except on coastal dunes which resemble heaths), this large grey butterfly remains the characteristic Brown of lowland heathland. Much more localised, and virtually confined to southern heaths, is the Silver-studded Blue. This beautiful Blue can occur in vast numbers after a fire or clearing, for the caterpillars feed on the tender growths of regenerating plants. Search also in moister areas where the heather has grown leggy.

Moors are similar to heaths, but occur at higher altitudes and mainly in the north, where the climate is colder and wetter. Bogs develop among poorly drained moorland, and can occur in small pockets on lowland heaths. These are waterlogged areas that are grassy round the edges, merging into wetter regions of pure moss that often surround open water. Moors and bogs dominate the sides of many mountains, but there may also be lush grassy meadows degenerating at high altitudes into a barren landscape of broken rocks.

The few butterflies that live in these upland habitats are adapted to withstand intense cold during winter and, in some cases, the prolonged submergence of their caterpillars. Some, like the Chequered Skipper, Marsh and Dark Green Fritillary have evolved beautiful races with large dusky wings that are better able to absorb the sun's rays.

The Large Heath is an attractive butterfly that lives only in the wettest acid bogs; search where Cotton Grass is abundant at all altitudes up to 800m. Less waterlogged areas, where Purple Moor Grass is dominant, are the habitat of the Marsh Fritillary, Chequered Skipper and Scotch Argus. These two latter butterflies are virtually confined, nowadays, to Scotland, and are found especially near plantations or among scrub, at altitudes of up to about 500m. Our most truly mountain species is the Mountain Ringlet which breeds only in lush meadows from 350-1000m high in the English Lake District and Scottish Highlands. Its very dark wings are particularly adept at absorbing the sun's warmth, as are those of another relic from the ice age, the Northern Brown Argus. This lives at lower altitudes, up to 350m, and is confined to well-drained base-rich northern hillsides, where Rockroses or Geraniums are common.

Northern
Brown
Argus

female

Silver-studded Blue

mating pair of
Silver-studded Blues

male

female

male

male

female

Mountain Ringlet

Graylings alighting on
a rock. When settled
they close their wings

GARDENS AND HEDGEROWS

Large numbers of adult butterflies are attracted to gardens, but the range of species is small because few are able to breed there. Since Browns, Skippers, Fritillaries, Hairstreaks and most Blues are reluctant to leave their breeding sites, it is unusual to see any in town or suburb, whilst country gardens only attract odd individuals from colonies that happen to occur nearby. However, all the more mobile species are attracted to flowers, notably the five common Vanessids (pages 22, 23). The Small Tortoiseshell is a particularly common visitor and often hibernates in cool lofts, garages or outhouses. All Whites except the Wood White are also attracted to gardens, and for both Large and Small Whites the vegetable patch is a major breeding ground. The Holly Blue is the only other species to breed significantly in gardens. Uniquely among British Blues, it is common in many suburbs, supported wholly by garden shrubs.

Hedgerows are much more important habitats. There is seldom an abundance of adults present, but the range of species can be considerable. Indeed, in flat landscapes, hedges and occasional woods are the main places left for breeding butterflies, whilst in Britain as a whole, the majority of Brown Hairstreak, Gatekeeper, Peacock, Comma, Holly Blue, Green-veined White, Orange Tip and Brimstone caterpillars feed either on hedgerow shrubs or on the ground plants beneath hedges. The Small Copper, Common Blue, several Skippers and other Browns also breed commonly along hedgerows.

The best hedges for butterflies are ancient boundaries that consist of a variety of shrubs growing above a sheltered bank or broad verge containing a rich ground flora. Spraying, ploughing, or burning the verge up to the edge greatly reduces the number of butterflies, as does frequent and severe trimming of the shrubs; tall unkempt hedges that are left two to four years between cuttings are ideal.

The Ice Plant (*Sedum spectabile*) is one of the best garden plants for attracting butterflies. Here you can see Small Tortoiseshells, two Painted Ladies and a Comma.

GARDENING FOR BUTTERFLIES

It is simple to attract all the species of mobile butterfly in the neighbourhood merely by growing their favourite nectar sources. It is very much harder to create suitable conditions for breeding (except for Holly Blue, Large and Small Whites), but well worth trying; even if you fail, Whites, Yellows and others will remain longer in the garden if their caterpillars' foodplants are present.

There are a few simple rules: try to create a suntrap where banks of flowers grow in full sunshine and yet have maximum shelter from the wind; only a limited range of garden flowers is really attractive to butterflies – aim for a succession of these from early spring until late autumn, and ensure that there is a profusion from mid-summer onwards when the Vanessids arrive to feed before hibernating; old fashioned varieties and species of plants are infinitely superior to most modern varieties. This is particularly true of the best of all butterfly plants, *Buddleia davidii*: the wild unkempt shrub with pale mauve flowers will fill any garden with the scent of honey and often be smothered with butterflies. Modern dark red and purple varieties are neater, but they are virtually scentless and seldom attract anything.

A definitive list of attractive plants is given in Matthew Oates' delightful book, *Garden Plants for Butterflies* (page 159). I recommend flowering Sallow (Pussy Willow), Snowdrop and Crocus for early Spring, followed by Wallflower, and wild species of Primrose, Bugle and Forget-Me-Not. Sweet Rocket is an excellent flower for all Whites, including Green-veined and Orange Tip, which may also be attracted, in diminishing order, by Horse Radish, Honesty, *Arabis*, and Aubretia. They will sometimes lay eggs, Green-veined on the leaves and Orange Tip on the flowers, of all these Crucifers.

By June and July, a good garden for butterflies should have Sweet William, Thyme and Candytuft in flower, followed by Applemint, Marjoram, Wild Hemp Agrimony (*Eupatorium cannabium*), Red Valerian, Lavender, and above all the two great shrubs: Buddleia and Hebe. The former will flower from mid-July until late September if some branches are pruned hard in Spring. Two essential plants for Autumn are Ice Plant (ensure that it is *Sedum spectabile*) and Michaelmas Daisy, whilst rotten fruit left lying on the ground is irresistible to Red Admirals.

Like it or not, any vegetable patch containing Brassicas will attract Small and Large Whites; Cabbage, Brussel Sprouts and also garden Nasturtiums are especially favoured for breeding. Brimstones have an extraordinary ability to find Purging and Alder Buckthorns; one bush in a hedge is ample and will attract many more adults in spring than garden flowers. Holly Blues seldom feed on flowers, but can be attracted to breed in any garden that has flowering (female) Holly in spring or ivy in summer. Variagated varieties of both are suitable, provided they flower and fruit. Finally, Stinging Nettle is invaluable as the foodplant of four Vanessids, but note that it is unlikely to be used unless growing on the sheltered, sunny side of a hedge or wall, and unless young growth is available; it is possible to create a succession of fresh leaves by occasional cuttings in spring and early summer.

Garden and Hedgerow Butterflies

Small Tortoiseshell caterpillar

Red Admiral

Peacock caterpillars are darker and have longer spines than the Small Tortoiseshell

Small Tortoiseshell

Peacock

Gardens are excellent places to see Vanessids: large butterflies with spectacular upperwings but sombre underwings that resemble bark or dead leaves. Up to five species can occur together in southern gardens, but only the Small Tortoiseshell, Peacock, and Red Admiral are common in the north. Vanessids are easy to identify and gather in gardens to feed on flowers, mainly from mid-summer to late autumn. Earlier in the year, more are seen along hedgerows and wood edges, where males establish territories and females search for egg sites. Peacock and Small Tortoiseshell caterpillars are simple to find, each in large dark groups on webs spun over Stinging Nettle leaves. Red Admiral and Comma caterpillars also feed on Nettles, but are solitary; the former lives in a folded leaf, the latter exposed on its plant, camouflaged like a bird dropping. The Painted Lady also breeds along hedgerows, but mainly uses Thistles.

The second commonest group of garden butterflies are the Whites. Only the Large and Small White, together known as Cabbage Whites, regularly breed there, and may be seen from spring until late autumn, reaching a peak in August. Orange Tips and Green-veined Whites are also frequent visitors, but although the male Orange Tip is unmistakable, females and Green-veined Whites are often overlooked as Small Whites; at rest, the green mottling or

Large White

Comma caterpillar

Painted Lady

Orange Tip

male

female

Comma

Green-veined White
caterpillar

caterpillar

female

Green-veined White

Gatekeeper

veins on their respective underwings make both easy to identify. Unless a Cabbage patch exists nearby, Orange Tips and Green-veined Whites are the commonest Whites seen along hedgerows for both breed on Crucifers growing at the base.

Hedgerows also support a succession of Browns, of which the Gatekeeper is the most characteristic species in the south. Smaller and brighter than the Meadow Brown, and with two rather than one white pupil in the large eyespot, it is often abundant in high summer and sometimes enters country gardens.

How to use the field guide

Fifty-eight species of butterfly, from seven different families, are regularly seen in Britain. On the whole, the members of each group share strong family characteristics and differ rather obviously from butterflies in different families. The main family groups are illustrated on this double page. For convenience, the large Nymphalid family has been split into two, and the Duke of Burgundy has been added to the Fritillaries, although it really belongs to a family on its own.

Having identified the family group from the illustrations on this page, turn to the appropriate identification notes and illustrations on the following pages. Here all the members of each group are illustrated lifesize, with notes pointing out features that help to distinguish between them. To fit them in, it has been necessary to depict most as set specimens that have been divided down the middle; the **upperwings are always shown to the left of the body, with the underwings separate on the right.**

Also included for each group is a chart of adult flight periods. The thickness of the red line represents the relative numbers of each species likely to be out through the summer months. Opposite this is a summary of each butterfly's status in the four countries. The symbols mean:

■ Common and widespread
▣ Local
◉ Scarce
○ Rare

When you have decided what you think the butterfly is, a page reference is given where a fuller description will confirm your identification or point you in another direction.

Illustrations on this page not to scale

Guide to the main Family groups

Skippers   Hesperiidae
Pages 26-27

Small and moth-like they live in discrete colonies in rough unfertilised grassland. Adults rarely stray and are often hidden among vegetation. Flight, when it occurs, is rapid and whirring, 'skipping' just above the grassheads. Most species have golden wings, but three are grey or chequered in black, white or yellow.

antennae held wide apart, usually hooked at tips

head as wide as body

large black eyes

large broad body

short stumpy wings, often held apart

Swallowtail   Papilionidae
Page   30

Large black and yellow with tails. Unmistakable.

Yellows and Whites   Pieridae
Pages 28-30

Medium sized to fairly large, with white or yellow wings, a few black marks, and a little green or orange in one or two species. The Marbled White (a 'Brown') and Swallowtail also fit this description, both are highly distinctive. True Whites have slow fluttering flights, all but Wood Whites roam fairly freely through the countryside, occurring in ones or twos in most habitats.

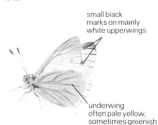

small black marks on mainly white upperwings

underwing often pale yellow, sometimes greenish

Copper, hairstreaks, blues
Pages 31, 32-33

Small butterflies, most with bright metallic colours. The Small Copper is unmistakable; 'Blues' include all butterflies with blue upperwings, though some females and a few males are brown. Coppers and Blues have numerous small spots on the underwings, all are active and conspicuous, and all except the Holly Blue live in discrete colonies in open, usually short, unfertilised grass or heathland. The Holly Blue wanders and prefers shrubs. Hairstreaks are elusive, living in small compact colonies, mostly on treetops. All except the Green Hairstreak have tails.

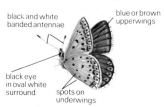

black and white banded antennae

blue or brown upperwings

black eye in oval white surround

spots on underwings

Fritillaries   Nymphalidae and Nemeobiidae   Pages 36-37

True Fritillaries are medium-sized to large butterflies with bright orange or golden upperwings criss-crossed by a network of black veins, crossbars, and often spots. The underwings are less golden but often intricately patterned; most species have bands of silver or white cells. They have a flitting flight. The Duke of Burgundy has a similar pattern, but is small with a whirring flight. All live in discrete colonies, mainly in woods.

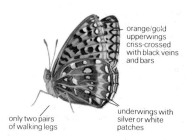

orange/gold upperwings criss-crossed with black veins and bars

underwings with silver or white patches

only two pairs of walking legs

The aristocrats: vanessids, emperor, admirals
Nymphalidae   Pages 34-35

Medium sized to large, with powerful flitting flights. Vanessids have indented wing edges and bright and gaudy upperwings, mainly coloured orange, black or red. Some also have small blue or white marks. The underwings are sombre, camouflaged to resemble bark or dead leaves. All are seen in small numbers in most habitats, including gardens. The Purple Emperor and White Admiral have large dark upperwings banded in white. They live in discrete colonies in large woods.

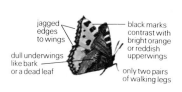

jagged edges to wings

black marks contrast with bright orange or reddish upperwings

dull underwings like bark or a dead leaf

only two pairs of walking legs

Browns   Satyridae
Pages 38-39

Small to fairly large, with a conspicuous black eyespot near the tip of the forewing on both sides. This nearly always has a white centre; similar eyespots often occur elsewhere on wings. The ground colour is generally tawny, light or dark brown, except on the Marbled White (black and white) and Wall Brown (golden, like a Fritillary with eyespots). Browns live in discrete colonies, usually in tall grassland, and flap lazily just above the grasslands.

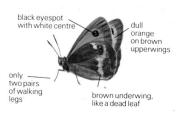

black eyespot with white centre

dull orange on brown upperwings

only two pairs of walking legs

brown underwing, like a dead leaf

Skippers

There are eight species. Narrow these down to four or fewer possibilities from the date and place; then decide between Group A or Group B and see opposite. Finally, check in the fuller accounts of individual species (pages 40-55).

MAR	APR	MAY	JUN	JUL	AUG	SEP	OCT/NOV		ENGLAND	WALES	SCOTLAND	IRELAND
						—		Grizzled	■	●		
						—		Dingy	■	■	●	●
								Chequered			○	
								Large	▨		●	
								Small	▨			
								Essex	■			
								Lulworth	○			
								Silver-spotted	○			

Group A

Bask with each fore and hindwing held together in the same plane, often flat. Predominantly dark wings with clearcut white or yellow markings in some species. Mainly May or June. Over by mid-July.

Group B

Bask with the forewings held aloft and the hindwings more horizontal. Predominantly golden wings with rather indistinct markings in some species. Rarely seen before June.

Group A

brown wings and fringe

black and white pattern on wings and fringe

◀ uniform underside

patterned underside

Dingy Skipper   Page 52

Grizzled Skipper   Page 54

yellow and black chequered pattern can be confused with the Duke of Burgundy

Central west Scotland only and the only Skipper in this region

Chequered Skipper   Page 40

Group B

tip of antennae orange underneath

long, thick, oblique scentmark (♂ only)

tip of antennae black underneath

short thin scent mark parallel to veins (♂ only)

clear gold upper and undersides in both sexes

Small Skipper   Page 42

Essex Skipper   Page 44

dull orange to olive upperparts

circle of gold spots

only found on the coast of Dorset, Devon, and Cornwall

♂

♀

Lulworth Skipper   Page 46

◀ faint pattern on underside

◀ greenish underside with silver spots

rare on chalk downs in S England

Large Skipper   Page 50

Silver-spotted Skipper   Page 48

Large Yellow and White Butterflies

See page 30 for chart of dates and status. Page 38 for Marbled White.

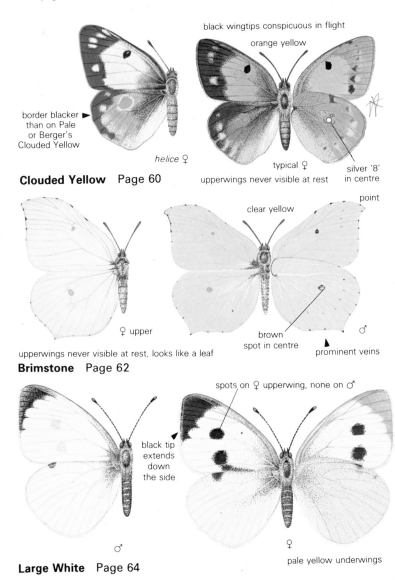

black wingtips conspicuous in flight

orange yellow

border blacker
than on Pale
or Berger's
Clouded Yellow

helice ♀

Clouded Yellow Page 60

typical ♀

upperwings never visible at rest

silver '8'
in centre

point

clear yellow

♀ upper

brown
spot in centre

prominent veins

♂

upperwings never visible at rest, looks like a leaf

Brimstone Page 62

spots on ♀ upperwing, none on ♂

black tip
extends
down
the side

♂

♀

pale yellow underwings

Large White Page 64

28

Medium-sized and Small White Butterflies

See page 30 for chart of dates and status

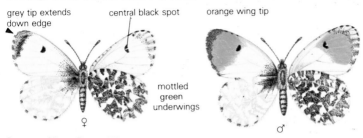

grey tip extends down edge

central black spot

orange wing tip

mottled green underwings

♀

♂

Orange Tip   Page 70

black tip on ♂ upperwing

unmarked oval underwings

upperwings never visible at rest

Wood White   Page 58

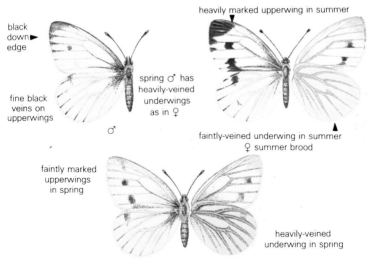

black down edge

heavily marked upperwing in summer

fine black veins on upperwings

spring ♂ has heavily-veined underwings as in ♀

♂

faintly-veined underwing in summer
♀ summer brood

faintly marked upperwings in spring

heavily-veined underwing in spring

♀ spring brood

Green-veined White   Page 68

Medium-sized and Small White Butterflies

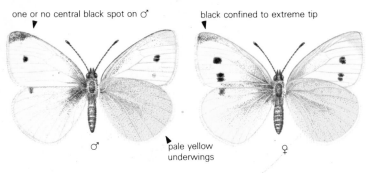

MAR	APR	MAY	JUN	JUL	AUG	SEP	OCT/NOV		ENGLAND	WALES	SCOTLAND	IRELAND
								Swallowtail	○			
								Brimstone	●	●		●
								Clouded Yellow	●	●	○	●
								Green-veined White				
								Small White				
								Orange Tip			▨	
								Large White				
								Wood White	○	○		▨

one or no central black spot on ♂

black confined to extreme tip

♂

pale yellow underwings

♀

Small White   Page 66

Swallowtail

Unmistakable. Found in Norfolk Broads only, except for rare escapes and vagrants

Swallowtail
Page 56

Small Copper and Hairstreaks

MAR	APR	MAY	JUN	JUL	AUG	SEP	OCT		ENGLAND	WALES	SCOTLAND	IRELAND
								Small Copper			■	■
								Green Hairstreak	■	■	●	●
								Black Hairstreak	○			
								White-letter H'stk	●	●		
								Purple Hairstreak	■	■	●	○
								Brown Hairstreak	●	●		○

gleaming copper upperwings

short tails

Small Copper Page 82

eye

♀ short tail

Purple Hairstreak Page 76

♂

♀ tail

Brown Hairstreak Page 74

angular wingtip ▶

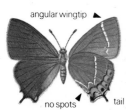

no spots ◀ tail

White-letter Hairstreak
Page 78

rounded wingtip ▶

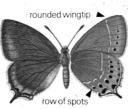

row of spots ◀ tail

Black Hairstreak
Page 80

tails short or absent

Green Hairstreak
Page 72

31

Blues

There are nine species, but consider the Large Blue extinct. All except Holly Blue are colonial, so usually males and females will both be present, looking different in most species. Upperwing colour is a poor guide except in male Adonis and Chalkhill Blues. Check upperwings for broad/narrow black borders, fringes for black veins, and underwings for absence (Group A) or presence (Group B) of orange, and the size and pattern of spots.

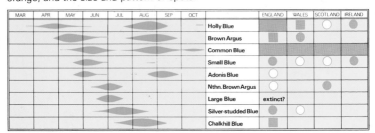

MAR	APR	MAY	JUN	JUL	AUG	SEP	OCT			ENGLAND	WALES	SCOTLAND	IRELAND
								—	Holly Blue			○	●
									Brown Argus	■	●		
									Common Blue				
									Small Blue	●	○	○	●
									Adonis Blue	○			
									Nthn. Brown Argus	○		●	
									Large Blue	extinct?			
									Silver-studded Blue	●	○		
									Chalkhill Blue	■			

Group A

No orange on under or upperwings.

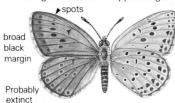

↗ spots

broad
black
margin

Probably
extinct

Large Blue   Page 156

silver underwings with minute black dots

♀ has brown
upperwings
with no blue

♂

Small Blue   Page 84

broad
black
margin

♀

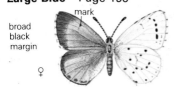

mark

round shrubs and in gardens

violet

chequered
upperwing
fringe ►

clear
hindwing
fringe ►

silver underwings with tiny black dots

♂

Holly Blue   Page 98

Group B

Orange mark on underwings and some upperwings.

no blue in either sex   no spot

orange
crescents

Brown Argus   Page 88

white spot usually present

clear ►
fringe

Brown Argus and
N. Brown Argus
never overlap in
flight period or
geographical
range

underwing spots may lack black centres

Northern Brown Argus   Page 90

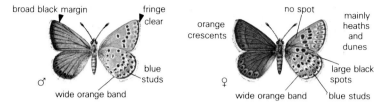

broad black margin

fringe
clear

orange crescents

no spot

mainly heaths and dunes

blue studs

large black spots

wide orange band

♂

♀

wide orange band

blue studs

Silver-studded Blue
Page 86

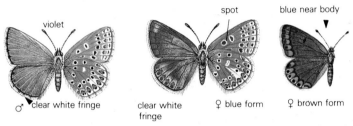

violet

spot

blue near body

♂ clear white fringe

clear white fringe

♀ blue form

♀ brown form

common in all habitats   all intermediates between brown and blue females exist

Common Blue
Page 92

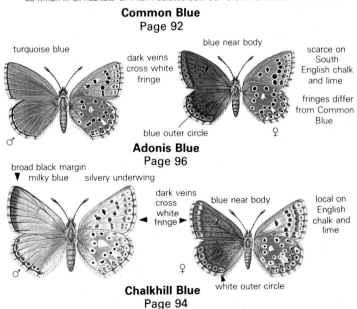

turquoise blue

dark veins cross white fringe

blue near body

scarce on South English chalk and lime

fringes differ from Common Blue

blue outer circle

♂

♀

Adonis Blue
Page 96

broad black margin
▼ milky blue   silvery underwing

dark veins cross white fringe ►

blue near body

local on English chalk and lime

♂

♀

white outer circle

Chalkhill Blue
Page 94

Emperor, Admirals and Vanessids

MAR	APR	MAY	JUN	JUL	AUG	SEP	OCT/NOV		ENGLAND	WALES	SCOTLAND	IRELAND
								Small Tortoiseshell				
								Comma		■		
								Peacock			●	■
								Large Tortoiseshell	○	○		
								Red Admiral			■	■
								Painted Lady	■	■	●	●
								White Admiral	■	○		
								Purple Emperor	●			

rounded wings

broad
white band across
dark upperwings

bright neatly
patterned
underwings

White Admiral
Page 102

pointed wings

purple in sunshine (♂)

♀ always brown

blurred
underwings

eye

Purple Emperor
Page 104

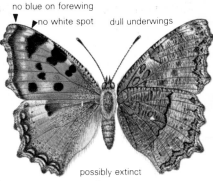

blue marks
white spot near tip
patterned underwings
no blue on forewing
no white spot
dull underwings

large black area

Small Tortoiseshell Page 110

possibly extinct

Large Tortoiseshell Page 112

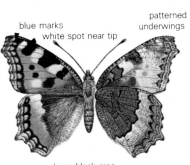

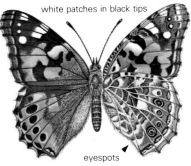

white patches in black tips

eyespots

Painted Lady Page 108

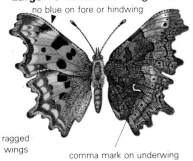

no blue on fore or hindwing

ragged wings

comma mark on underwing

Comma Page 116

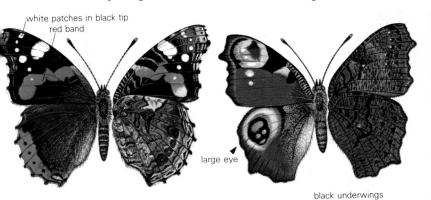

white patches in black tip
red band

Red Admiral Page 106

large eye

black underwings

Peacock Page 114

35

Medium-sized Fritillaries

MAR	APR	MAY	JUN	JUL	AUG	SEP	OCT		ENGLAND	WALES	SCOTLAND	IRELAND
								Pearl-bordered	●	●	●	○
								Duke of Burgundy	●			
								Marsh	●	■	●	●
								Small pearl-bordered	●	■	■	
								Glanville	○			
								Heath	○			
								Dark Green	●	●	●	●
								High Brown	○	○		
								Silver-washed	●	■		●

spots on upper forewing

sharp ◀ black veins

▼ six or seven silver pearls

six silver patches

Small Pearl-bordered Fritillary
Page 118

spots on upper forewing

seven ◀ silver pearls

two silver patches

Pearl-bordered Fritillary
Page 120

◀ no spots on any wing

one band of white cells on underwing
very rare in SE and SW England

Heath Fritillary
Page 132

spots on tip

bright underwings

two rows of spots

black spots in orange circles
Isle of Wight only

Glanville Fritillary
Page 130

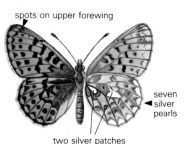

◀ no spots on tip

one row of spots on dull ◀ underwing

size varies

black dots in orange boxes

Marsh Fritillary
Page 128

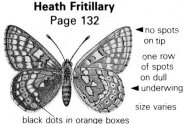

spots on all edges

two bands of white cells on underwing

Duke of Burgundy
Page 100

Large Fritillaries

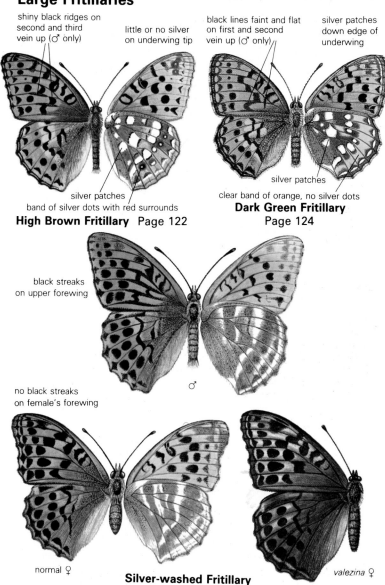

shiny black ridges on second and third vein up (♂ only)

little or no silver on underwing tip

black lines faint and flat on first and second vein up (♂ only)

silver patches down edge of underwing

silver patches

band of silver dots with red surrounds

High Brown Fritillary Page 122

silver patches

clear band of orange, no silver dots

Dark Green Fritillary Page 124

black streaks on upper forewing

♂

no black streaks on female's forewing

normal ♀

Silver-washed Fritillary Page 126

valezina ♀

37

Browns

MAR	APR	MAY	JUN	JUL	AUG	SEP	OCT		ENGLAND	WALES	SCOTLAND	IRELAND
								Speckled Wood			■	
								Wall Brown			●	■
								Small Heath				
								Meadow Brown				
								Mountain Ringlet	○		○	
								Large Heath	●	●	■	●
								Marbled White	■	●		
								Ringlet			■	
								Gatekeeper				●
								Grayling	●	●	●	●
								Scotch Argus	○		■	

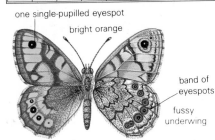

one single-pupilled eyespot
bright orange
band of eyespots
fussy underwing

Wall Brown   Page 136

one single-pupilled eyespot
brown and cream
blurred underwing

Speckled Wood   Page 134

Marbled White
Page 142

unmistakable black and white chequered pattern, see Whites page 28

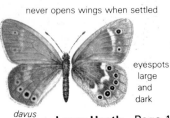

never opens wings when settled

davus form

eyespots large and dark

scotica form

Large Heath   Page 152

almost no trace of eyespots ◄

never opens wings when settled
one single-pupilled eyespot ▼

white dots

Small Heath   Page 150

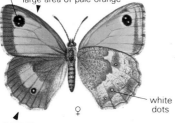

one double-pupilled eyespot
large area of pale orange

white dots

♀

eyespot

male scent mark

Gatekeeper or Hedge Brown Page 146

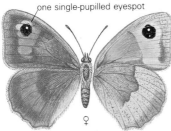

one single-pupilled eyespot

♀

less orange than Gatekeeper

eyespot small on ♂

♂

black dots

plain brown hindwing

Meadow Brown Page 148

two single-pupilled eyespots

never opens wings when settled
Grayling Page 144

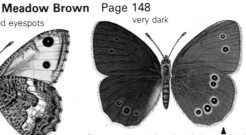

very dark

five eyespots with yellow halos on hindwing
Ringlet Page 154

faint eyespots with no white pupils
northern mountains only
Mountain Ringlet Page 138

two single ► pupilled eyespots form '8'

north only
Scotch Argus Page 140

CHEQUERED SKIPPER
Carterocephalus palaemon

LIFE CYCLE

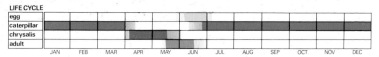

	JAN	FEB	MAR	APR	MAY	JUN	JUL	AUG	SEP	OCT	NOV	DEC
egg												
caterpillar												
chrysalis												
adult												

Adult identification

Average wingspan 29mm (♂) to 31mm (♀)

Our only Skipper with a really distinct chequered pattern on the upperwings; note the bright orange yellow marks among a blackish-brown background and broad veins. The female has paler marks, but the sexes are similar: the underwings show the same clear pattern, but are duller with a greenish-grey ground colour.

In England, the Duke of Burgundy (page 100) is superficially similar in markings, size and flight, and is often mistaken for this species. At rest, the Duke of Burgundy is distinguished by a row of black spots on an orange background along all the wing edges, and its neater bands of white marks on the under hindwings. Some Carpet Moths

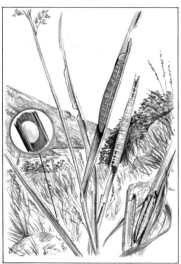

are also similar in flight. On the continent, it may be confused with the Northern Chequered Skipper and the beautiful Large Chequered Skipper.

Young stages

The **egg** is globular and shiny white with fine reticulations. It is laid singly on a blade of Purple Moor Grass or Wood False Brome and is difficult to locate.

The **caterpillar** lives in a tube formed from whichever grass the egg was laid upon, the edges being bound together by stout silk cords. The blade is eaten above and below the tube, leaving it isolated on the midrib and easy to spot from July onwards. By October, the fully fed caterpillar is green, with dark green and white lines and a pale green head. It hibernates, fully fed, in a tent of leaf blades and gradually turns straw coloured.

The **chrysalis** is formed in spring in a new tent of dead leaf blades. It is well camouflaged, being pale buff coloured with dark lines.

Habitat and behaviour

The adults live in small isolated colonies, and are easy to miss except in the finest weather. In England, they were once found in sunny woodland rides, clearings, and rough sheltered grassland adjoining woods, where the caterpillars fed almost wholly on Wood False Brome (*Brachypodium sylvaticum*). This grass is sometimes used in Scotland, but Purple Moor Grass (*Molinea caerulea*) seems to be the main foodplant North of the Border. Search for Scottish colonies in sunny scrubby areas, often on the edges of copses or in sheltered combes. In Scotland the eggs are laid on small clumps of grass, half-shaded by Bog Myrtle and other shrubs; the large

A female of the rare Chequered Skipper in a Scottish glade. It is the most distinctively marked of all the Skippers.

exposed tussocks of Purple Moor Grass that grow in open damp rank grassland or moorland are invariably ignored.

The adults are rather inconspicuous, but in fine weather bask with their wings wide open, and the males establish perching posts on small prominent shrubs in sunny nooks. From these they make the typical short buzzing flights of Skippers, chasing females and visiting flowers.

Distribution and status

This is a rare butterfly. It once occurred, very locally, in several woods in north Lincolnshire and the east and southern English Midlands, but all English colonies are now believed to be extinct, the last survivors being recorded in the mid 1970s in Rockingham Forest and other woods near Peterborough. Although several surveys have been made, it is possible but unlikely that a small English colony has been overlooked, but note that the Duke of Burgundy, with which it may be confused, occurs on several former sites.

The Chequered Skipper was not discovered in Scotland until 1942, when a colony was found near Fort William, Inverness. Several more have been discovered very recently over a considerable area of Inverness and Argyll, and today one can guarantee to see it

on a number of sites in this region, given suitable weather. It is not thought that the butterfly has spread or increased, merely that it had been overlooked. It is worth searching any patch of suitable habitat in this region rather than confining oneself to the well known colonies.

Solid colour: confirmed range

SMALL SKIPPER *Thymelicus sylvestris*

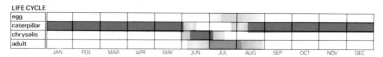

LIFE CYCLE

	JAN	FEB	MAR	APR	MAY	JUN	JUL	AUG	SEP	OCT	NOV	DEC
egg												
caterpillar												
chrysalis												
adult												

Adult identification

Average wingspan 30mm

The sexes are similar in size and appearance, apart from a black scent line across each upper forewing on the males (page 27). The upperwings are bright orange-brown, with faint black veins and black margins. The underwings are a dull orange-brown, tinged with grey-green, and are not patterned.

The Essex Skipper often flies with this butterfly and is almost identical. It is usually necessary to net and examine the undersurfaces of the tips of the antennae: these are deep black on the Essex Skipper, as if dipped in ink, but reddish-orange on the Small Skipper (page 27). The male Small Skipper also has a longer bolder scent mark that runs obliquely, rather than parallel to

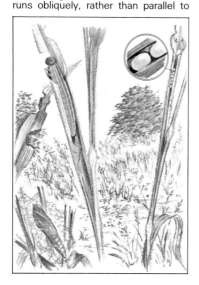

the upper wing edge. See also the male Lulworth Skipper (page 27) which is smaller and less golden. No other species in Europe is similar to these three.

Young stages

Three to five smooth, pale yellow, flattened oval **eggs** are laid in a row inside the sheath of a tall grass stem, usually Yorkshire Fog. These are quite easy to find.

The **caterpillars** hibernate together without feeding in minute silk cocoons spun in their grass sheath. In spring they disperse and live alone in rolled leaf blades fastened into a tube by silk cords. The caterpillar leaves wedge-shaped notches after feeding on other blades, which are easy to spot in May. When fullgrown, it often rests exposed on leaf blades and has a green head, with a pale green body marked by darker lines on top.

The **chrysalis** is waxy green, paler on the abdomen, and has a short pink beak on the head. Look for it in a loose cocoon of coarse silk netting and grass leaves.

Habitat and behaviour

The Small Skipper forms discrete colonies from which the adults rarely stray. In the south, it occurs in most places where Yorkshire Fog and wild grasses are allowed to grow tall, but it is easy to miss a small colony because the adults frequently rest among dense vegetation. Small colonies are often found along thin strips of land, such as road verges and hedge banks. Larger numbers breed along most woodland rides and edges, whilst vast populations often develop in rough abandoned or disturbed grassland.

On most sites, the main or only

42

A male Small Skipper in his typical basking posture. This Skipper may be confused with the similar Essex Skipper, but for the reddish-orange undersides to its antennae.

food of the caterpillar is Yorkshire Fog (*Holcus lanatus*), although breeding sometimes occurs on Timothy (*Phleum pratense*) and Wood False Brome (*Brachypodium sylvaticum*). The female chooses tall mature clumps around which she makes a circling buzzing flight, before crawling up and down the flowering stems, probing the loose sheaths to find one that is suitable for her eggs. Although Yorkshire Fog is eliminated from intensively cultivated fields, it is common still in rough grassland, wasteland and woodland on all soils.

Distribution and status

The Small Skipper is one of the commonest and most widely distributed butterflies on all soils throughout southern England and most of Wales, but there is a clearcut northern limit to its range. It is absent from the north of England, Scotland and Ireland. In the south, numerous colonies have been eliminated through intensive farming and the removal of hedgerows, especially in flat landscapes, but it is still to be expected almost anywhere where Yorkshire Fog grows in tall clumps within its range.

On the continent, it is also common and virtually ubiquitous in rough grassland throughout central and southern Europe, but is absent from Scandinavia and much of the north.

Solid colour: confirmed range

ESSEX SKIPPER *Thymelicus lineola*

LIFE CYCLE

	JAN	FEB	MAR	APR	MAY	JUN	JUL	AUG	SEP	OCT	NOV	DEC
egg												
caterpillar												
chrysalis												
adult												

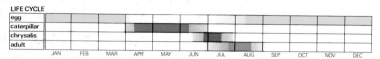

Adult identification

Average wingspan 27mm (♂) to 30mm (♀)

The wing markings in both sexes are almost identical, with the male scent mark no more than a fine black line across his upper forewing. The ground colour is bright orange-brown on the upperwings, with faint black veins and black wing margins. The underwings are dull orange-brown tinged with grey-green, and are plain.

Essex and Small Skippers are indistinguishable in flight and very similar at rest: see pages 27 and 42 for distinguishing features. These two skippers fly together on many sites, the Essex emerging one to two weeks later, but with a considerable overlap. Unless egglaying is seen, it will be necessary to examine the tips of the antennae.

Young stages

A short row of smooth milk-white **eggs** is laid within firm flower sheaths on coarse grasses. Each is flat, like that of the Small Skipper, but more oval in outline. It also differs from the latter species by hibernating as an egg.

Like the Small and Lulworth Skipper, the **caterpillar** lives mainly in a folded blade of grass, fastened by stout silk cords to form a tube. It feeds on a wide range of coarse grasses (see Habitat). The full grown caterpillar is pale green, striped with dark green down the back and yellow along the sides. The head differs from the Small Skipper's in being striped with pale brown.

The **chrysalis** occurs in a coarse net-like tent of silk spun between folded grass blades. It is yellow-green, and the beak is white, not pink as in the Small Skipper.

Habitat and behaviour

Like all our 'golden' Skippers, the Essex flies and breeds in self contained colonies and is rather easy to overlook. Colonies should be sought in rough, tall grassland, including isolated strips such as hedgerows, road verges and the rides and edges of woods. Vast numbers occur on some abandoned or lightly grazed chalk grassland, but it is also common on some acid soils, as well as among the wetlands and salt marshes of East Anglia, where it was originally discovered. The range of coarse grasses eaten by the caterpillar is unknown, but Cocksfoot (*Dactylis glomerata*) and Creeping Soft Grass (*Holcus mollis*) are the main species, with Timothy (*Phleum pratense*) probably important in some habitats. Caterpillars are occasionally found also on Wood False Brome (*Brachypodium*

44

The female of this mating pair of Essex Skippers has her wings open, whilst the male shows the black tips of his antennae that distinguish Essex from Small Skippers.

sylvaticum) and Tor Grass (*B. pinnatum*), but not on Yorkshire Fog, the foodplant of the Small Skipper. Breeding everywhere is confined to tall mature clumps of these grasses.

The adults spend long periods at rest, perched on warm patches of bare ground or amongst dense vegetation. In full sunshine they make short, rapid skipping flights, at grass head height buzzing from flower to flower.

Distribution and status

The Essex Skipper is confined to England, south of the Wash. Colonies — some huge — are common in rough grassland and saltmarshes throughout East Anglia, Kent, Surrey, Sussex, and the east Midlands, and also on Salisbury Plain. Its status elsewhere is poorly known because few naturalists bother to check small Skippers in western and central counties; it is always worth doing so. It does however seem to be a genuine rarity in Dorset, although present on the coast, and scattered colonies occur in Cornwall, Devon and probably Avon. Although reputedly spreading westwards, the Essex Skipper may always have bred in western counties, but have been overlooked in the past.

In Europe, the Essex Skipper is common in central and southern regions, and occurs over a wider range than the Small Skipper, for example in Sweden.

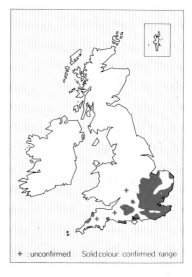

+ : unconfirmed   Solid colour: confirmed range

LULWORTH SKIPPER *Thymelicus acteon*

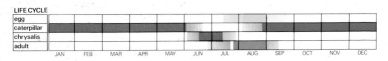

LIFE CYCLE

	JAN	FEB	MAR	APR	MAY	JUN	JUL	AUG	SEP	OCT	NOV	DEC
egg												
caterpillar												
chrysalis												
adult												

Adult identification

Average wingspan 25mm (♂)
to 27mm (♀)

The smallest and darkest of the 'golden' Skippers, the upperwings are dun or olive-brown, dusted with gold, with black margins. The female is lighter and has a distinct circle of gold rays on the upperside of each forewing (like the eye of a peacock's feather), which reflects the sun. This pattern is faintly visible on some males (page 27), which also have a black scent bar across each forewing. The underwings of both male and female are uniformly straw coloured.

The female Lulworth Skipper is distinguished from Large and Silver-spotted Skippers by the 'peacock's feather' of gold marks, its much smaller size, and plain underwings. The male is smaller and darker than the Small or Essex Skipper and the undersurface of each antenna is cream coloured.

Young stages

Up to fifteen, but usually five or six, pale yellow oval **eggs** are laid in a row in the flower sheaths of Tor Grass, especially in dead brown growth. Look for them in August when they are quite easy to find.

The **caterpillars** hibernate without feeding, in a row of tiny white cocoons spun where the eggs were laid. They disperse in April to live alone in tubes of folded Tor Grass blades fastened double by silk. At dusk each caterpillar eats the blade above and, eventually, below it, making distinctive V-shaped notches and later leaving the tube isolated on the midrib. This is very easy to find in June. The caterpillar is up to 25mm long, pale green with dark green and cream stripes. That of the Essex Skipper has brown stripes on its head, whilst the Small Skipper caterpillar is dark green down its back.

The **chrysalis** is hard to find in a loose cocoon of grass and silk near the ground. It is about 17mm long, with pale green head and wings, bright green thorax, and yellow-green abdomen. The beak on the head is twice as long as that of the Small Skipper.

Habitat and behaviour

This is a butterfly of warm south-facing rough hillsides, clifftops, and under-cliffs. It is restricted to base-rich soils near the south coast, where Tor Grass (*Brachypodium pinnatum*) is abundant. However, breeding occurs only where this coarse grass grows both in dense mature clumps, at least 20cm tall, and in sunny sheltered spots. Most broken

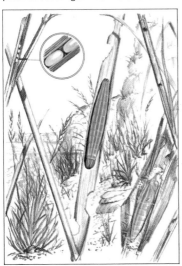

A female Lulworth Skipper feeding on the Isle of Purbeck on the Dorset coast. Note the golden 'peacock eye' on the upper forewing which shines in the sunlight.

undercliffs and some abandoned hillsides in southeast Dorset contain acres of this habitat, where the Lulworth Skipper is extraordinarily abundant, the adults jostling for nectar on Marjoram, Thistles and other flowers right down to the shore line. Much smaller colonies inhabit the grazed and exposed hillsides in this region, breeding in scattered patches where tall clumps of Tor Grass grow in sheltered spots beside stone walls, amongst scrub, or in abandoned pits. Flights are brief, rapid and buzzing, like all the 'golden' Skippers.

Distribution and status

There are about ninety British colonies of the Lulworth Skipper. Nearly all are in southeast Dorset, where it breeds almost continuously along the coast between Swanage and Weymouth on all chalk and limestone cliffs and undercliffs. There is another string of colonies one to five miles inland, running parallel to the coast along a south-facing escarpment of steep chalk downs. Many inland colonies are small, but on abandoned hillsides and on the undercliffs some populations of several hundred thousand adults occur. It is especially abundant to the east and west of Lulworth Cove, after which it was named. Elsewhere, a few small colonies exist on the south coast at Burton Bradstock, Dorset, southeast Devon, and near Polperro, Cornwall.

The old Torquay colonies are probably extinct, but there is little doubt that this skipper has increased enormously in recent years in other parts of its restricted range. It has benefited from the lack of grazing by rabbits following myxomatosis and subsequent invasion of coarse grasses, a process that has been so harmful to other butterflies.

Solid colour: confirmed range

SILVER-SPOTTED SKIPPER
Hesperia comma

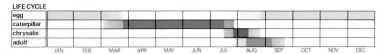

LIFE CYCLE

	JAN	FEB	MAR	APR	MAY	JUN	JUL	AUG	SEP	OCT	NOV	DEC
egg												
caterpillar												
chrysalis												
adult												

Adult identification

Average wingspan 30mm (♂)
to 36mm (♀)

The underwings are the most distinctive feature of both sexes, and give this Skipper its name: they are olive-green and marked with conspicuous silver patches. The upperwings have gold or yellow marks on a dark brown background. The contrast is greater in the female, which has brighter marks and a deeper ground colour. The male is much smaller and has a black bar of scent scales across each upper forewing.

Old faded Large Skippers (page 50) can survive to September and are often mistaken for this butterfly. In flight they are identical, although young Large Skippers are more golden. At rest, the undersurfaces appear very different,

with only a faint ginger and gold pattern and no silver on the Large Skipper. No other Skipper on the continent closely resembles either of these species, but see the female Lulworth Skipper which, although tiny, has somewhat similar upperwings (page 46).

Young stages

The **egg** laid singly, is quite large (about 0.7mm high) and is easy to find if suitable Sheep's Fescue (see Habitat) is examined in late summer or autumn. It is yellow-white, smooth and shaped like a tiny pudding-basin placed upside down on the side of a leafblade.

The **caterpillar** is difficult but not impossible to find, living solitarily in a small tent of Sheep's Fescue leaves spun together by silk. It has an olive-green, wrinkled grub-like body, up to 25mm long, with a black head.

The **chrysalis** is formed in a tough cocoon at the base of grass stems and is even harder to find than the caterpillar. It is pale olive-brown with much darker head, thorax and wing cases, and the whole surface is covered with short bristles.

Habitat and behaviour

This is a sun-loving butterfly that is restricted to the hottest parts of Britain. It occurs in discrete colonies, mainly on the steep, thin-soiled, south-facing slopes of southern chalk downs. The caterpillars feed solely on Sheep's Fescue (*Festuca ovina*). This fine leaved grass is still abundant on many un-fertilised downs, but only certain plants are acceptable: egg laying is confined to small isolated tufts growing beside bare ground especially, in sunny depressions, such as hoofprints. The size of a colony is directly related to the

The beautiful Silver-spotted Skipper was named after the silver spots on its greenish underwings. It is now rare and is in some danger of extinction.

amount of *suitable* Sheep's Fescue present. Today, most warm downs are too overgrown to support colonies of this Skipper, whilst on marginal sites, breeding is confined to a few sparse 'islands', such as path edges. Good sites, with thousands of adults, contain several acres of short Sheep's Fescue growing very sparsely amongst crumbly chalk scree.

The adults tend to be inconspicuous even on the best sites because they are inactive unless the air temperature exceeds 20°C, and even then spend long periods out of sight, basking in pockets of bare ground. Flight is short and rapid, buzzing just above the close cropped turf between a wide range of chalk flowers.

Distribution and status

This is one of our rarest butterflies. Colonies once bred on many base-rich hillsides up to Yorkshire, but apart from one limestone site in Somerset, they are now restricted to a few isolated areas of chalk, mainly on steep escarpments in the south Chilterns, N. Dorset, Hampshire, south Sussex, and on the North Downs between Guildford and Reigate and in southeast Kent. Many colonies disappeared following the collapse of rabbit grazing due to myxomatosis in the 1950s to '70s, but, with the partial return of rabbits, a few old sites have been reoccupied. There are now about 50 colonies; most are small but some contain several thousand adults.

On the continent, the Silver-spotted Skipper is widely distributed and especially common on chalk and limestone in warm regions, where it breeds in more overgrown conditions than in Britain.

Solid colour: confirmed range

49

LARGE SKIPPER *Ochlodes venata*

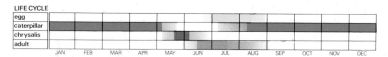

LIFE CYCLE

	JAN	FEB	MAR	APR	MAY	JUN	JUL	AUG	SEP	OCT	NOV	DEC
egg												
caterpillar												
chrysalis												
adult												

Adult identification

Average wingspan 33mm (♂) to 35mm (♀)

A sturdy Skipper with long antennae, distinctly clubbed at the tips. The upperwings are brown around the edges with large bright orange patches towards the body, divided by black veins. This pattern is clearer in the female, whilst the male has a large black scent line across the middle of each upper forewing. The underwings are duller in both sexes, with a faint pattern of orange patches against a greenish-brown background. This is the only common Skipper with orange and brown patterned wings. The rare Silver-spotted Skipper has similar upperwings but distinct silver patches on the under-wings (page 48); the female Lulworth Skipper (page 46), though much smaller, is superficially similar. No additional continental species resembles these three, but note that the Silver-spotted Skipper is as common as the Large Skipper in central Europe.

Young stages

The **egg** is dome shaped in profile, circular from above, and quite large (0.8mm high). It is pearl white, and is laid singly under the leaf blades of Cocksfoot or, sometimes, False Brome. It is not easy to find.

The **caterpillar** feeds on grass, living in a blade held double by little ropes of silk to form a tube, or sitting exposed on a leaf when full grown. It hibernates, half grown, in a sturdier tent of several leaf blades, and resumes feeding in spring. Fairly easy to find, the caterpillar is blue-green when full grown, with a dark green line down the centre and a cream coloured line along each side. The head is dark.

The **chrysalis** is very dark, especially on the head, thorax and wing cases, with a waxy bloom. Search for it in its silk and grass blade tent in early June.

Habitat and behaviour

The Large Skipper lives in distinct colonies in a wide range of rough places where wild grasses grow un-checked. The usual foodplant is Cocksfoot (*Dactylis glomerata*), although False Brome (*Brachypodium sylvati-cum*) is sometimes used and can possibly support a colony. In either case, tall clumps growing in sunny sheltered positions are used for breeding. Look for colonies in un-improved grassland, along hedgerows and road verges and, especially, on the edges, rides and glades of woods and in rough scrubby places: it prefers

The male Large Skipper perches alone with his wings held apart waiting for passing females. It is a common butterfly throughout the lowlands of England and Wales.

more sheltered sites than the Essex or Small Skipper, although all three are often found together.

The adults fly only in sunshine and, like most Skippers, appear to buzz and skip above the grassheads. They frequently land on shrubs, especially the males which establish individual perching posts on prominent leaves in sunny corners, from where each sorties after passing females in rapid swirling flights. Between flights he will usually return to the same leaf, and can then be closely observed.

Distribution and status

The Large Skipper is absent from Ireland and is a scarce butterfly in Scotland, occurring locally only in the southwest corner. Further south it is absent at high altitudes in the Lake District, Pennines, and Welsh mountains, but is otherwise one of the commonest species throughout all lowland areas of England and Wales. There can be little doubt that numerous colonies have disappeared in recent years, due to the intensification of agriculture, the shadiness of modern forestry plantations, and the general tidying up of the countryside; nevertheless, colonies are still to be expected wherever extensive clumps of Cocksfoot and tall wild grasses occur.

The Large Skipper is also very common throughout much of Europe, extending well into Norway and Sweden. It is absent, however, from southern Spain.

Solid colour: confirmed range

DINGY SKIPPER *Erynnis tages*

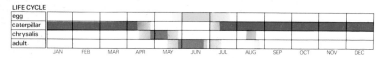

LIFE CYCLE

	JAN	FEB	MAR	APR	MAY	JUN	JUL	AUG	SEP	OCT	NOV	DEC
egg												
caterpillar												
chrysalis												
adult												

Adult identification

Average wingspan 29mm

Both sexes of this moth-like Skipper look much the same. The upperwings are mainly grey-brown, with a blurred pattern on the forewings of darker patches and shiny areas, and an oily looking sheen in sunshine. Tiny white dots embellish the outerwing edges of all wings and the fringes are pale grey. There is some variation in the strength of this pattern, and old adults look truly dingy and very pale. The underwings are light grey-brown, unmarked except for small white dots. Although it is easy to identify in Britain, beginners some-times confuse Dingy and Grizzled Skippers (page 54): the latter has a much more contrasting pattern, especi-ally on the underwings, and distinctly chequered black and white fringes.

Young stages

The **egg** is dome shaped in profile, round from above, and has several distinct ribs running from the summit to the base. Although pale when laid, it soon turns bright orange and is easy to find on Bird's-foot Trefoil, Greater Bird's-foot Trefoil, or Horseshoe Vetch. Search on the upper surfaces in the groove where the leaves join the stem, or on the tenderest young leaflets.

The **caterpillar** feeds on vetch leaves and lives alone in a loose tent of its foodplant spun near the ground. It can be found, with practice, in midsummer; the caterpillar is then full grown and uniformly green with a purplish-black head. It hibernates in a more substantial tent from late July onwards.

The **chrysalis** is formed in the hiber-nation tent in spring. The dark green thorax and wing cases contrast with a warm chestnut-coloured abdomen.

Habitat and behaviour

Nearly all colonies of Dingy Skipper breed on Bird's-foot Trefoil (*Lotus corniculatus*) and are found where this vetch grows in abundance in sunny sheltered places. The best sites are dunes and rough ground round the coast, and ancient chalk and limestone downs where the turf is open or fairly short; Horseshoe Vetch (*Hippocrepis comosa*) is also eaten on these latter sites. Smaller colonies occur also on heaths, embankments, wasteland, and disturbed or rough ground that is not too overgrown to suppress the food-plant. In woods, there may be small numbers along the broad mown rides of modern plantations, in areas of young coppice, or in damper glades where Greater Bird's-foot Trefoil (*L. uliginosus*) grows.

The Dingy Skipper emerges in spring and is the most moth-like of all the butterflies found in the British Isles. Like all Skippers they only fly in sunshine.

This butterfly lives in small self-contained colonies which typically contain tens rather than hundreds of adults. The males congregate in sheltered hollows or at the base of hills and, on sunny days, both sexes spend long periods basking on patches of bare ground, with the wings held wide apart, pressed against the warm soil. Flight is swift, whirring just above the ground. At night and in cool weather, they perch on dead flowers or grass-heads around which they drape their wings, looking very like moths.

Distribution and status

This is the only Skipper to be found in Ireland, where it is widely but very locally distributed and is frequent only in the Burren; curiously, it is absent from most of the Irish coastline. In Scotland, a few colonies breed in the northeast (much further north than other Skippers) and there are more along the southwest coast. The coastline of England and Wales also supports a string of colonies which, although not occurring continuously, may be encountered almost anywhere except along flat muddy stretches such as around the Wash. Inland colonies are nowadays much more localised in England and Wales. They occur most frequently on downs and in woods in southern counties and become distinctly scarce north of the Chilterns and

the Cotswolds. Colonies are absent from high altitudes.

In short this is our most widely distributed Skipper, although nowhere is it anything like so common as Large, Essex or Small Skippers are in the south. This was not always true of some southern counties, but countless inland colonies of the Dingy Skipper have recently been lost due to the intensified use of land for agriculture and forestry.

+ : unconfirmed   Solid colour: confirmed range

GRIZZLED SKIPPER *Pyrgus malvae*

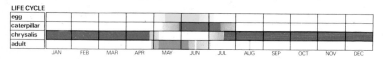

Adult identification

Average wingspan 27mm

Both sexes look much the same and are best distinguished by the shorter stumpier body of the female. On the uppersides, the wings are a checkerboard of black and white markings and the fringes have conspicuous black and white bars. The undersides are similar, but duller, and the hindwing has large white marks on a greenish background (see page 27). It is unlikely that any other British butterfly will be confused with this species except, possibly, the Dingy Skipper (see pages 27 and 52). Certain day-flying moths look similar in flight, and on the continent, there are 19 other extremely similar Skippers which can be identified only by netting and reference to a European guide.

Young stages

The **egg** is pale green, fading to white, and dome-shaped with about 20 ribs running from the summit to the base. About 0.5mm tall, it is laid on the underside, and occasionally upperside, of a small leaf of its foodplant (see Habitat), and is possible, but not easy to find.

In July, the tiny yellow **caterpillar** rests under fine silk along the midrib of the upperside of the leaf, leaving blotches on the leaf where it has fed; it is quite easy to find. When older, it has a dark green body with brown stripes (much darker than the Dingy Skipper caterpillar) and a black head. It lives in a loose tent formed by drawing the edges of a leaf around itself.

The **chrysalis** is chestnut-brown with contrasting white wing cases. It occurs in a loose cocoon of neat silk netting spun near the base of its foodplant. It may be found from autumn onwards.

Habitat and behaviour

The caterpillars feed on the leaves of several members of the Rose family, usually Wild Strawberry (*Fragaria vesca*) or Creeping Cinquefoil (*Potentilla repens*), with Tormentil, Agrimony and Blackberry (short, stumpy bushes only) less often used. It lives in small discrete colonies which rarely consist of more than a hundred adults. These are found where their foodplants grow in sunny sheltered places, usually among sparse, but not necessarily very short vegetation. Typical sites are recent clearings, broad rides and the edges of woods; rough sheltered grassland among scrub, especially on chalk and limestone downs; and any warm crumbling bank.

The adult is an active little butterfly

A Grizzled Skipper basks with its wings wide open in the sunshine. When in flight the chequered wings blur making it hard to follow.

with a darting flight that is hard to follow due to the blurred effect of the chequered wings. However, it frequently alights, often on bare ground, and may be closely approached as it sits basking with its back towards the sun. As with the Dingy Skipper, a few adults occasionally emerge to form a partial second brood during August.

Distribution and status

Like the Dingy Skipper, with which it often flies, numerous inland colonies of the Grizzled Skipper have disappeared in recent years due to the increased shadiness of woods, the intensification of agriculture, and the tidying up of the countryside. Moreover, its foodplants are much less common along the undisturbed coast than the Dingy Skipper, being mainly confined to cliffs and undercliffs. Today, the Grizzled Skipper is local but not rare in central southern counties of England, but is much scarcer both in the southwest and north of the Cotswolds and Chilterns. In the Midlands and East Anglia it is now mainly confined to larger woods, and its range just extends into Yorkshire. It is absent from Ireland, extinct in Scotland, and very rare in Wales apart from a few scattered colonies on scrubby cliffs along the coast.

Solid colour: confirmed range

55

SWALLOWTAIL *Papilio machaon*

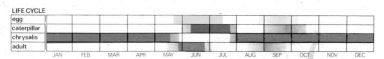

LIFE CYCLE

	JAN	FEB	MAR	APR	MAY	JUN	JUL	AUG	SEP	OCT	NOV	DEC
egg												
caterpillar												
chrysalis												
adult												

Adult identification

·Average wingspan 80mm (♂)
to 90mm (♀)

Both sexes of this very large and unmistakable butterfly are similar. Note the long tails below a blue border containing an orange eye, and the bold black and pale yellow markings of the wings. These, however, blur into the colour of weak tea when the Swallowtail is in flight. No other British butterfly is remotely similar. The British Swallowtail belongs to a subspecies that is unique to this country. Continental Swallowtails are paler, with thinner black borders and veins. There is also another Continental species, the even larger Scarce Swallowtail, which is not scarce at all and has vertical black stripes on a paler background.

Young stages

The globular **egg** is pale yellow at first, but turns brown after a few days. It is laid singly on the caterpillar's foodplant, Milk Parsley, and is quite easy to find. Search the forked leaves of prominent plants in the Norfolk Broads in June.

The **caterpillar** too can be found by searching suitable Milk Parsley in summer. At first it looks like a small bird dropping: black and spiny with a white band. When older it is smooth and plump, beautifully striped with black on a fleshy-green background. It has an unusual way of deterring enemies: a large orange horn (the osmeterium) is extruded from a fold behind the head, and gives off an unpleasant smell.

The colour of the **chrysalis** varies from green to pale grey with black marks. It is hard to find on reed stems or its foodplant. A few hatch to form a partial second brood of adults each summer, but the majority hibernate.

Habitat and behaviour

The British subspecies of the Swallowtail requires extensive areas of wetlands and fens, and is now confined to the Norfolk Broads. The caterpillar's only foodplant is Milk Parsley (*Peucedanum palustre*). Robust, tall, flowering specimens are selected for egglaying, and these grow only in the wettest marshes, especially where the reedbeds are kept open by regular cutting. In many places, the Broads are becoming too dry and overgrown for this butterfly, but fortunately suitable conditions are deliberately maintained on some nature reserves.

The Swallowtail is a magnificent insect, with a powerful gliding flight, and can still be seen quite regularly over the open water as it flies from one reedbed to the next.

The Swallowtail, the British Isle's most spectacular butterfly, perching on Milk Parsley in the Norfolk Broads.

The paler Continental subspecies of the Swallowtail is much more mobile and breeds on a range of Umbellifers in other habitats. It occasionally reaches southern counties and establishes itself for a year or two on chalk downs breeding mainly on the Wild Carrot (*Daucus carota*).

Distribution and status

Colonies of the British Swallowtail once bred throughout the fenlands of Cambridgeshire and east Lincolnshire, and perhaps in other wetlands in the south, but all were destroyed when these areas were drained. The last fenland colony survived until the 1950s on a nature reserve at Wicken, near Cambridge, but even this became unsuitable as neighbouring land was drained. The Swallowtail is now confined to the Norfolk Broads, where it is still quite widespread. It is numerous, locally, around a few marshes where suitable conditions have been maintained; one can still see it in these places.

Occasional single individuals may also be seen elsewhere in Britain, mainly near Butterfly Farms from which they periodically escape. Migrants from the continent are very rarely encountered on southern chalk downs, mostly in Kent and Dorset.

Solid colour: confirmed range

WOOD WHITE *Leptidea sinapis*

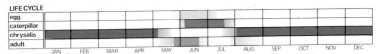

	JAN	FEB	MAR	APR	MAY	JUN	JUL	AUG	SEP	OCT	NOV	DEC
egg												
caterpillar												
chrysalis												
adult												

Adult identification

Average wingspan 42mm

This is our smallest White butterfly and one of the easiest to identify. When settled, the wings are never opened, so only the underwings are seen. These are long, thin and oval – quite different from the rounded shape of other Whites. The ground colour is a yellowish-white on which are darker patches, but no real pattern, of grey-green scales. A green tinge is particularly noticeable on Irish specimens. The dainty flight of this butterfly is idiosyncratic and easily identified: the wings are flapped so slowly that you can clearly see black tips to the male's upper forewings against a clear white background. On females, these tip markings are little more than a dusting of grey scales. During spring, inexperienced butterfly watchers often mistake unusually small, weak-flying male Green-veined Whites for this scarce butterfly. The differences are obvious when they settle (page 68).

Young stages

The **egg** is bottle shaped, off white, and somewhat glassy in appearance. It is laid on the undersurfaces of vetch leaves, on plants growing proud above the surrounding vegetation in sunny sheltered spots, and can be found quite easily, with practice, in June.

The **caterpillar** feeds on vetch leaves and is possible to find when full grown in July. It is tubular in shape and pale green, with a darker green stripe running down its back and a yellow stripe along each side.

The pretty pointed **chrysalis** is green with pink streaks, but is almost impossible to find among the dense vegetation in which it hibernates.

Habitat and behaviour

This delicate little butterfly rarely strays from its discrete colonies. These are few and far between, but on good sites may contain thousands of adults. Look for colonies where there is an abundance of the caterpillar's foodplants – Meadow Vetchling (*Lathyrus pratensis*), Bitter Vetch (*L. montanus*), Tufted Vetch (*Viccia cracca*) and Bird's-foot Trefoil (*Lotus corniculatus*) are favourites – and where these grow as tall bushy plants projecting above other vegetation in sunny sheltered places. Typical sites are recently cleared woods that are beginning to grow up again, ditches and scrubby edges to broad sunny rides in young plantations, overgrown sheltered fields besides woods, scrubby broken undercliffs, and abandoned railway cuttings.

Whatever the habitat, males are extremely conspicuous as they flap and

This female Wood White is curving her abdomen to lay a minute egg on a Vetch leaflet. The caterpillar feeds on the Vetch leaves and is easily spotted when full grown in July.

flutter almost in slow motion, sometimes hovering a foot or two above the ground, at other times patrolling rides and clearings in a systematic quest for a female. The female flies less often, but when seen, is just as weak and fragile as the male. In warm years, there is a partial second brood of adults in summer, but essentially this is a springtime butterfly.

Distribution and status

The Wood White is a widespread and fairly common butterfly in Ireland, and can be encountered in almost any scrubby or woodland area throughout. It does not occur in Scotland, and is a scarce insect in England and Wales, now reduced to around 90 sites. Colonies may be found, very locally, in plantations and railway cuttings throughout the southern English Midlands, the Wye Valley, and east Wales. A few breed in the west Weald of Surrey and Sussex, one or two in Hampshire, Dorset, and Wiltshire, and slightly more in Somerset and Devon, notably on the coast. This butterfly was much more widespread and common in the 19th century, but has declined drastically since coppicing was abandoned in most woodlands. There has been a slight recovery and spread into young plantations and abandoned railways in recent years, often helped by deliberate reintroductions.

+ : unconfirmed   Solid colour: confirmed range

59

CLOUDED YELLOW *Colias croceus*

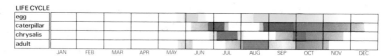

	JAN	FEB	MAR	APR	MAY	JUN	JUL	AUG	SEP	OCT	NOV	DEC
egg												
caterpillar												
chrysalis												
adult												

Adult identification

Average wingspan 57mm (♂)
to 62mm (♀)

When settled, the Clouded Yellow hardly ever opens its wings so normally only the underwings are seen. These are deep yellow, with a black spot half-way across the forewing. In the centre of each hindwing is a pair of silver spots surrounded by reddish brown forming a conspicuous figure of 8. Yellow-green eyes peer out from a yellow head and body. The butterfly is usually seen in rapid flight, thus revealing rich orange upperwings with broad black borders that cannot be confused with any other species. There is, however, a pale form of the female, called *helice,* in which the orange ground colour is replaced by grey. It is quite common in some years and looks

identical, in flight, to the Pale Clouded Yellow and Berger's Clouded Yellow (page 158), which are always much rarer than *helice.* Note that the black border on *helice* is darker and broader on the hindwing and extends further round the lower edge of the forewing (page 28).

Young stages

The **egg** is bottle shaped and pale yellow when laid, but turns pink then orange after a day or two. It is laid singly, usually in mid June, often on the uppersides of legume (Clover, Lucerne and Trefoil) leaves, and is not too difficult to find in 'Clouded Yellow Years'.

The **caterpillar** is very hard to spot among its leguminous foodplants. It feeds on the leaves and, when fully grown, is dark green with a yellow line along each side with orange circles round the spiracles.

The **chrysalis** is pale yellow-green, but is well hidden and unlikely to be found.

Habitat and behaviour

The Clouded Yellow is a migratory butterfly that is unable to survive British winters, except possibly the mildest, and then only in insignificant numbers. Winter breeding occurs round the Mediterranean. Each spring the off-spring fly north through Europe, to reach Britain's southern shores in highly variable numbers every year. These spread northwards in diminishing numbers occasionally reaching Scotland. Flight is powerful and rapid, but they also linger awhile when breeding sites are encountered. These can be cultivated fields sown with clovers or Alfalfa, whilst unsprayed flowery down-

The Clouded Yellow with its yellow wings and silver 'figure of eight' in the centre forming an attractive contrast to its green eyes and pink legs.

land, with an abundance of Trefoils or Vetches, is also a favourite habitat. In addition to these concentrations, roaming adults may be seen, usually singly, in any other habitat, including gardens.

Distribution and status

The distribution and abundance of the Clouded Yellow varies enormously from one year to the next, depending largely on how many immigrants arrive in spring. In some years there are almost none, but normally one expects to see this butterfly in ones and twos on southern downs in high summer. Occasionally there is a large immigration, which breeds up to produce extraordinary numbers in the second brood. The butterfly is then a common sight throughout the countryside of southern England, Wales and Ireland, whilst smaller numbers penetrate into northern England and even Scotland. These 'Clouded Yellow Years' are few and far between nowadays. The last, in 1983, occurred unexpectedly after a 35 year gap.

Immigrants are occasionally seen in May and early June. The second brood is much larger.

Solid colour: confirmed range

61

BRIMSTONE *Gonepteryx rhamni*

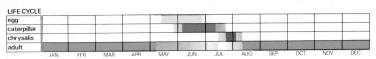

LIFE CYCLE

	JAN	FEB	MAR	APR	MAY	JUN	JUL	AUG	SEP	OCT	NOV	DEC
egg												
caterpillar												
chrysalis												
adult												

Adult identification

Average wingspan 60mm

The Brimstone is a fairly large butterfly and one of the easiest to identify. The male has clear yellow wings which, in flight, can be mistaken only for the Clouded Yellow. The latter is smaller, darker, and a deeper orange-yellow. The female Brimstone has much paler upper wings compared to the male, with a green tint that, at a distance can easily be misidentified for a Large White (page 28). Both sexes are unmistakable at rest. They always sit with their wings closed, so only the undersides are seen. These look extraordinarily like a pale yellow leaf, with pointed corners, prominent veins, and even a spot of 'mould' in the centre. The body and legs are the same pale yellow, but the eyes are large, black and shiny. Note, too, the beautiful clubbed antennae which sprout from between the eyes like a pair of pink stalks.

Young stages

The **egg** is off-white and bottle shaped. It is very easy to find in late spring, singly, on Purging Buckthorn and Alder Buckthorn bushes. Search beneath the tenderest young leafshoots on the tips of branches growing in sunny situations.

The **caterpillar** is just as easy to spot and at all ages, for it sits exposed along the midrib of a leaf, leaving obvious feeding damage on the leaves around it. It is tubular with a white stripe and bluish-green tinge that blends well with the colour of its background.

The **chrysalis** is fleshy green with purple marks and curiously leaf-like. It is usually formed on nearby vegetation, and very hard, but not impossible to find.

Habitat and behaviour

The Brimstone is a conspicuous butterfly of woods, hedgerows and scrubby places. The adults emerge in August, and immediately prepare for hibernation by gorging themselves on nectar, sometimes continuing well into November. They do not live in compact colonies, but wander through the countryside, often entering gardens to feed. Although usually seen in ones or twos, scores sometimes gather on Teasels and Thistles along woodland rides in late summer. Hibernation occurs mainly in woods, deep among evergreens such as Holly and Ivy.

The adults re-emerge on the first warm days of spring and again roam, this time in search of mates and egg-laying sites. Females have an extra-

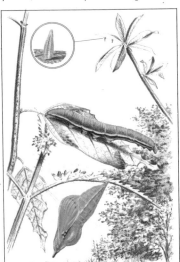

The Brimstone has distinctive pink antennae. Perching with its wings closed, as here, it has a marvellous leaf-like camouflage.

ordinary ability to find even the most isolated of Buckthorn bushes; Purging Buckthorn (*Rhamnus cathartica*) and Alder Buckthorn (*Frangula alnus*) are equally acceptable. Both grow in scrub, along wood edges and rides, and less often, in hedges, Brimstones are sure to be found wherever these foodplants are common.

Distribution and status

The Brimstone's range coincides almost exactly with that of its two foodplants. It is common through most of southern England up to Humberside, breeding on Purging Buckthorn on calcareous and neutral soils, and on Alder Buckthorn in wetter, peaty or acidic areas. The most northern sites are in the Lake District, although strays reach Scotland. In Wales it is an extremely local species, except in the southwest and near the southern coast. Although peat bogs abound in Ireland, Alder Buckthorn is rare, hence the Brimstone is mainly found in the limestone areas breeding on Purging

Buckthorn. It is, however, a reasonably common butterfly around the Burren and in central counties.

+ : unconfirmed   Solid colour: confirmed range

63

LARGE WHITE *Pieris brassicae*

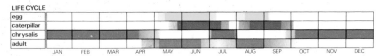

	JAN	FEB	MAR	APR	MAY	JUN	JUL	AUG	SEP	OCT	NOV	DEC
egg												
caterpillar												
chrysalis												
adult												

Adult identification

Average wingspan 63mm (♂)
to 70mm (♀)

The upperwings of this large butterfly are gleaming white, with conspicuous black tips to the forewings. The female also has a pair of black spots in the middle of each forewing and a black smear along the lower edge (page 28). These marks are slightly greyer in the spring brood. The underwings are pale yellow dusted with grey, and have no pattern.

Size alone distinguishes the Large White from our other white butterflies, but note that the female Brimstone looks similar in flight (page 62). The occasional small individual may be distinguished from the Green-veined White and female Orange Tip by its unpatterned underwings, whilst the dark tip on the upper forewing of the

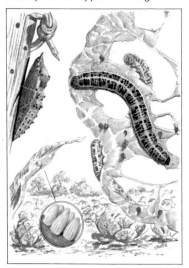

Small White is confined to the extreme tip, and does not extend down the outer edge (page 66). In addition, the male Small White has a black spot in the centre of the forewing.

Young stages

The **eggs** are yellow, bottle shaped and laid in neat groups of 50-100 on the leaves of Cabbages and other food-plants, usually on the undersides. They are very easy to find.

The **caterpillars**, too, are extremely conspicuous. At first pale green, they turn a mottled grey-green when full grown with black splodges and short white hairs, and smell most unpleasant. They live gregariously exposed on Brassica plants, which can be stripped to a skeleton of veins and smelly droppings.

The **chrysalis** is grey-green with yellow and black marks. It hibernates, and can often be found, under window ledges, on walls, sheds and fences.

Habitat and behaviour

Adult Large Whites may be seen anywhere, but are commonest around vegetable gardens, allotments and cabbage fields. They will breed on any species of Brassica and on garden Nasturtiums, but cultivated Cabbages and Brussel Sprouts are its favourites.

The Large White is a highly mobile butterfly with a powerful, if somewhat fluttering flight. It does not live in identifiable colonies but flies throughout the country breeding wherever suitable conditions are encountered. In some years home bred populations are boosted by vast swarms from the Continent, and there may be return flights too, with emigrants teeming towards France.

There are generally two generations of adults a year, with the second

The male Large White has neat black tips to his forewings but lacks the wing-spots found on females.

emergence in high summer always the most numerous. After warm summers there is often a partial third brood which lasts well into October.

Distribution and status

The Large White is one of the commonest butterflies throughout the British Isles. It reaches our remotest islands, including the north Shetlands, although its survival in northern localities may be dependent on immigrants and its appearance there is consequently more erratic. It may be expected in all habitats and at all altitudes.

Numbers have always fluctuated greatly from one year to the next, but in the past it regularly occurred in devastating swarms. This is most unusual nowadays, since numbers have been depleted by a virus disease and are controlled by insecticides. Parasitic *Apanteles* wasps also kill countless caterpillars in some years.

Solid colour: confirmed range

SMALL WHITE *Pieris rapae*

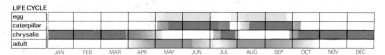

	JAN	FEB	MAR	APR	MAY	JUN	JUL	AUG	SEP	OCT	NOV	DEC
egg												
caterpillar												
chrysalis												
adult												

Adult identification

Average wingspan 48mm

This is the smaller of the two 'Cabbage' Whites that are common garden pests; other features that distinguish it from the Large White are described on page 64. The underwings of both sexes are dull pale yellow, dusted with grey, and differ greatly from the patterned underwings of our two other medium-sized White butterflies: the Green-veined White and female Orange Tip (page 29). The upperwings of the Small White are clear white (except in Ireland where they may be yellowish) with black markings that differ slightly between the sexes and in the two generations. The first brood, in spring, is much more faintly marked. The males, indeed, may be pure white, but usually the summer markings of dark

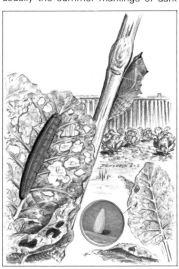

wingtips, dark scales near the body, and a black spot in the middle of the forewing can be seen as faint grey marks. The female has all these marks plus an extra spot on the upper forewing and a faint grey streak along its lower edge.

Young stages

The **egg** is pale yellow, bottled shaped, and simple to find beneath the leaves of Brassicas (especially Cabbages) and wild Crucifers in April. Although laid singly, there may be several eggs on the same plant, but not the massive clusters of the Large White.

The **caterpillar** lives solitarily, boring first into the heart of its Brassica to feed, then long after the damage has been done, emerging to rest openly along the midribs of leaves. It is then easy to find, although dark green and well camouflaged against its background.

The **chrysalis** varies from being clear green to pale brown with dark speckles. It can sometimes be found on sheds, fences and under windowsills in similar positions to the Large White chrysalis.

Habitat and behaviour

Like the Large White, this attractive butterfly is a familiar sight around Cabbage patches, allotments and vegetable gardens, and is widely despised as an agricultural and garden pest. However, although its caterpillars undeniably inflict severe damage on cultivated Brassicas, and even on garden Nasturtiums, many also feed on wild Crucifers along hedgerows and in wood edges.

The Small White does not live in proper colonies, but ranges widely over town and countryside, laying eggs wherever its foodplants are found. It

The Small White, showing its yellowish underwings and indistinctly marked wingtips. Like the Large White, its caterpillars are a familiar pest in cabbage patches throughout Europe.

prefers plants that are slightly sheltered, so Cabbages growing near hedgerows towards the edges of fields and, especially, in gardens are chosen. Large clusters of adults may gather in these situations, otherwise the butterfly is normally seen in ones and twos flying almost anywhere. Both sexes are attracted by white flowers when feeding. Numbers are invariably higher in the second generation and vary greatly from one year to the next. In some years their numbers are supplemented by large migrations from the continent, and after some warm summers there may be a small third brood of home bred adults lasting well into autumn.

Distribution and status

This is a very common butterfly that may be found almost anywhere in England, Wales and Ireland. It is equally common in southern Scotland, but becomes much more localised on the mainland in the north. It seldom if ever reaches the outer Isles, such as Shetland and the Outer Hebrides, but is common on islands in the south such as the Isle of Man, Isle of Wight, Anglesey and the Scillies.

Solid colour: confirmed range

67

GREEN-VEINED WHITE *Pieris napi*

LIFE CYCLE

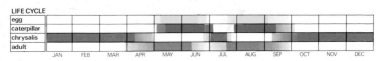

	JAN	FEB	MAR	APR	MAY	JUN	JUL	AUG	SEP	OCT	NOV	DEC
egg												
caterpillar												
chrysalis												
adult												

Adult identification

Average wingspan 50mm but smaller adults are common.

This common, medium-sized White butterfly looks very like a Small White when flying, but at rest broad grey-green stripes along the veins of the underwings distinguish it from all other butterflies. This veining, which gives the butterfly its name, is highly conspicuous on all adults except for second (summer) brood females, when it is rather faint (page 29).

When the wings are open, note that the tips of the upper forewings have dark marks extending further down the outer edge than on the Small White (page 30), and that the veins are picked out as fine grey lines on all adults except first (spring) brood males. Upperwing markings are always heavier on second brood adults: the males then have a spot in the middle of each forewing whilst the females have two large spots, the lower of which merges with a black streak along the forewing's lower edge, rather like a miniature female Large White (page 28).

Young stages

The **egg** is pale, bottle shaped and laid singly. It can be found quite easily on the undersurfaces of wild Crucifer leaves, often on small plants and usually in damp places.

The **caterpillar** is dark green, with yellow rings round the spiracles but lacking the yellow stripe found on the Small White's caterpillar. Although well camouflaged, given persistent searching it can be discovered feeding on the stems and leaves of its foodplant.

The **chrysalis** is formed out of sight among dense vegetation. It comes in various colour forms ranging from green to pale brown, but all are well camouflaged and difficult to find.

Habitat and behaviour

The Green-veined White has a weak fluttering flight, but is nevertheless quite mobile. In most regions it does not live in identifiable colonies, but flies over wide areas searching for mates and breeding sites. However, unlike our two Cabbage Whites, it is not a true migrant; odd individuals may be seen flying across any habitat, even dry heaths and open chalk downland, but by and large they congregate around their breeding sites. There, at best, it will be seen in hundreds, especially in the second (August) brood which is the most numerous. In the south, there are usually two broods of adults which overlap and may be seen any time from late April to September, peaking in late

The spectacular underwings of the Green-veined White are clearly visible as it feeds on nectar. The black wingtips, extending down the edge of the forewing, can just be seen.

May and, dramatically, in early August. There is occasionally a small third brood in late September. At high altitudes and on northern Islands, there may only be a single emergence in June and July.

Search for them in damp, uncultivated places, such as boggy meadows, riversides, ditches, lush hedgebanks and verges, and the rides and edges of woods. The caterpillars feed on a range of Crucifers growing in humid spots, including Water Cress (*Nasturtium officinale*), Lady's Smock (*Cardamine pratensis*), Garlic Mustard (*Alliaria petiolata*) and Hedge Mustard (*Sisymbrium officinale*).

Distribution and status

The Green-veined White is frequently overlooked due to its similarity to the Small White. It is, in fact, one of our commonest and most widely distributed butterflies, although absent from the Shetlands and some areas of the central and northwest Highlands on the Scottish mainland. On a local scale, it has undoubtedly suffered greatly in recent years from drainage and agricultural improvements. Even so, small numbers survive along ditches, banks and swampy corners, even in the most intensively cultivated regions.

Solid colour: confirmed range

69

ORANGE TIP *Anthocharis cardamines*

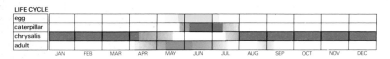

	JAN	FEB	MAR	APR	MAY	JUN	JUL	AUG	SEP	OCT	NOV	DEC
egg												
caterpillar												
chrysalis												
adult												

Adult identification

Average wingspan 45mm (♂)
to 50mm (♀)

The male Orange Tip is unmistakable: a medium sized White butterfly with bright orange wingtips. The female is less conspicuous, with grey-black tipped wings instead of orange, and a large black spot in the centre of each upper forewing. On the undersides, the hindwing is similar in both sexes, with a mottled, moss green pattern, looking like lichen against a white background (pages 23, 29).

In flight, the female looks very like a Small or Green-veined White, but is slightly greener. At rest, her underwings are unmistakable, and neither of these other Whites has her black central spot on each upper forewing. On the continent, there are several species of Orange Tip, whilst the 10 species of Dappled or Bath Whites resemble the female.

Young stages

The **egg** is bottled shaped and very easy to find in late May and June. It is laid singly beneath flowerbuds on the caterpillar's foodplants, and is white at first but soon turns bright orange.

The **caterpillar** is long, thin and tubular, pale orange with black hairs when young, but eventually becoming blue-green on top and dark green underneath, with inconspicuous hairs. It lies along the top of a seedpod of its foodplant and, although beautifully camouflaged, is easy to find at all ages through June and early July.

The caterpillar leaves its plant to pupate among dense vegetation, and the **chrysalis** is almost impossible to find. It has an elegant triangular shape and is normally pale brown, although sometimes clear green.

Habitat and behaviour

The greatest concentrations of both sexes of Orange Tip are seen where there is an abundance of the caterpillar's food, which is the flowers and seedpods of tall Crucifers. Much the commonest plants used are Lady's Smock (*Cardamine pratensis*) and Garlic Mustard (*Alliaria petiolata*). The former grows mainly in damp places and on heavy soils, often in tall open grassland and in woodland rides; the latter prefers drier conditions along hedgerows, banks, wood edges, and wasteland, especially on calcareous soils. Between them, these Crucifers support Orange Tips over a wide range of habitats, although boggy meadows with abundant Lady's Smock are scarce nowa-

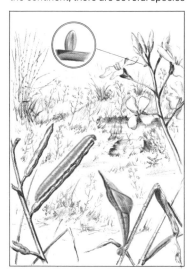

A freshly emerged male Orange Tip perches on one of the caterpillar's principal foodplants, Lady's Smock. Only the male has orange wingtips.

days, and the grubbing up of hedge-rows has greatly reduced Garlic Mustard in some flat regions. Additional foodplants are Hedge Mustard and, less often, Charlock, Watercress, and Honesty.

Adult Orange Tips are quite mobile. They are not confined to self-contained colonies, and the males may be seen almost anywhere within their range, flitting slowly between white objects in their quest for females. The latter are more secretive (and often dismissed as Small Whites), but their roamings are betrayed by the presence of eggs even on the remotest and most isolated of foodplants.

Distribution and status

Despite some local declines, the Orange Tip is a common butterfly throughout Ireland, Wales, and England, except for the northeast, where it is mainly confined to damp valleys. In Scotland it is distinctly local in the south, and absent from the Highlands and all of the Isles. It is, however, well distributed over a large area in northeast Scotland where it may, indeed, be spreading.

On the continent it is also a common butterfly throughout most countries.

Solid colour: confirmed range

GREEN HAIRSTREAK *Callophrys rubi*

LIFE CYCLE

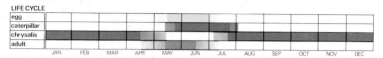

	JAN	FEB	MAR	APR	MAY	JUN	JUL	AUG	SEP	OCT	NOV	DEC
egg												
caterpillar												
chrysalis												
adult												

Adult identification

Average wingspan 33mm
(15mm closed)

An unmistakable little butterfly that always sits with its wings closed, displaying their bright green undersides. Small areas of the plain brown uppersides are sometimes visible where the wings overlap. The tail is reduced to a stump in this hairstreak, and the two sexes look much the same. In flight (page 16), the impression is of brown blurred wings, rather like a Dingy Skipper or female Blue, but at rest it is unmistakable.

In southeast France, Chapman's Green Hairstreak is slightly larger, with a white line across the green undersides, but is otherwise almost identical.

Young stages

It is almost impossible to find wild **eggs,** which are glassy, pale green, flattened spheres inserted singly into the tender leaf tips or flower buds of the foodplants.

The **caterpillar,** when fullgrown, is shaped like a large fleshy woodlouse, with distinct segments. It is green with yellow markings, and is hard to spot even though it lives openly among the young leaf or flower tips of its various foodplants.

Secretions make the ground-living **chrysalis** attractive to ants, but it is very hard to find except, by chance, under flat stones containing ant nests. It is deep brown and quite hairy.

Habitat and behaviour

The Green Hairstreak is found in many habitats, including moorland, lowland heath, chalk and limestone downs, woods, embankments, and rough scrubby wasteland. Typical colonies contain fewer than 50 adults. The eggs are laid on a wide range of plants, from low-growing herbs to shrubs. The main foods are Bilberry (*Vaccinium myrtillus*) on moors, Gorses (all *Ulex* spp.) on acid and neutral soils, and Rockrose (*Helianthemum chamaecistus*) on calcareous grassland. Dyer's Greenweed, Bird's-foot Trefoil, and Dogwood and Buckthorn flowers are often used elsewhere. The common feature of most sites is that they contain scattered shrubs and are warm and sheltered; many are hillsides.

The males are territorial and perch in the sunshine on prominent shrubs, usually one per bush, in the lowest parts of sites, where they await the females. It is always easy to find the males by examining suitable bushes. When disturbed, they are hard to follow

The Green Hairstreak is conspicuous when perching on Bluebells or other spring flowers, but is beautifully camouflaged when it settles on leaves.

for they make rapid jerky flights among the shrubs, but invariably return to the same perches and can then be closely approached. The females are much less obvious, and fly inconspicuously over larger areas to lay their eggs.

Distribution and status

This is our most widely distributed Hairstreak. Colonies may be expected in suitable habitat throughout Ireland, west Wales, southwest England and west Scotland, where it remains a local, yet common butterfly; huge populations occasionally develop in warm Gorse-filled valleys and on some Bilberry moors. Elsewhere in Britain the Green Hairstreak has become much more localised, although it is still frequently encountered in most southern English counties, especially on heaths. In central and eastern England, it is reduced to a handful of colonies per county, mostly around woods or on embankments.

The Green Hairstreak was very much commoner until quite recently, but countless colonies have been lost through the reclamation or improvement of old grassland, heaths and moors, through intensive forestry, and the general tidying up of the country-side. Throughout Europe, it remains a common butterfly of seminatural habitats.

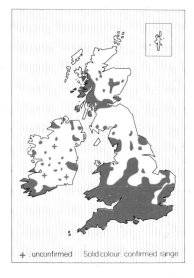

+ : unconfirmed   Solid colour: confirmed range

73

BROWN HAIRSTREAK *Thecla betulae*

LIFE CYCLE

	JAN	FEB	MAR	APR	MAY	JUN	JUL	AUG	SEP	OCT	NOV	DEC
egg												
caterpillar												
chrysalis												
adult												

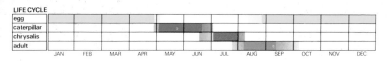

Adult identification

Average wingspan 38mm (♂) to 40mm (♀)

Adults are usually seen with the wings closed, exposing bright golden underwings crossed by two thin white lines, and a distinct tail. The female is a richer gold and has the longer tail. Brown Hairstreaks open their wings in weak sunshine: the upperwings are deep brown, marked on the forewings with faint yellow patches in the male or large orange blotches in the female.

No other butterfly is similar seen close up or at rest, but the male Gatekeeper (page 146), flying high among the treetops, can be mistaken for this species. The Gatekeeper is less golden and has a slower, less erratic flight. A more usual mistake is to misidentify the male Vapourer moth, which is bright

gold but smaller, and flies by day in a similar manner among treetops in late summer. It is much commoner than the Brown Hairstreak. Confirm by searching for Brown Hairstreak eggs in winter.

Young stages

The presence of this butterfly is most easily established by searching for the pin-head sized **egg,** which is laid singly or in pairs, and looks like a tiny white bun. This is very conspicuous against the dark bark of young prominent Blackthorn twigs; examine the bases of spines, or forks and notches during winter.

The **caterpillar** has a slug-like shape in profile, but is triangular when seen head on. It is pale green with yellow stripes, and is perfectly camouflaged as it rests, upside down, beneath a Blackthorn leaf. It can be found quite easily by patient searching in late June.

The dark brown, featureless **chrysalis** is almost impossible to find. It is formed on the ground among leaf litter or in crevices, and is sometimes tended by ants.

Habitat and behaviour

Colonies are found mainly in well wooded districts, especially on heavy soils, or in slightly hilly areas where there are numerous small hedged fields containing a high proportion of Blackthorn among the shrubs. Typical colonies are quite small and are centred on a wood, where the adults congregate for mating year after year on the crown of a tall prominent 'master' tree, often an Ash. The males rarely descend, or indeed fly, obtaining their food from aphid honeydew on the treetops. After mating, the females soon disperse to lay their eggs, singly, low down on

The Brown Hairstreak is an elusive butterfly, but the female is sometimes seen when she rests on Blackthorn leaves between bouts of egglaying.

Blackthorn (*Prunus spinosa*) or any other *Prunus* they encounter. They fly over a very wide area around the master tree, laying at low densities on young prominent growths along wood edges and, particularly, hedges. Nearly all the adults seen will be egglaying females, but even these are secretive, flying seldom and even then hugging the hedgerows. The egg, on the other hand, is very easy to find in the first months of winter after the leaves have fallen. By spring most will have been destroyed by hedge trimming.

Distribution and status

The Brown Hairstreak is a scarce butterfly that has disappeared from many regions, but is often overlooked. In Ireland, it is well distributed around the Burren but probably, nowadays, nowhere else. It is also extinct in Scotland and northern England. There are, however, two areas of abundance in southern England, and another in Wales, where eggs may be expected on any suitable-looking hedge. Look for it in Wales in the little wooded valleys throughout the southwest, and in England in a band of similar habitat across north Devon and into Somerset, in the vales between Exmoor and Dartmoor. The third concentration is in the West Weald of Surrey and Sussex, among the extensive woods on the clays.

Elsewhere, occasional colonies survive in southern English counties, mainly on heavy soils, but very few survive north of the Oxford/Buckinghamshire border, except in a pocket of north Lincolnshire. Numerous extinctions have occurred in the flatter parts of southern England, notably in East Anglia. These, no doubt, are victims of the loss of hedgerows and other scrubby areas.

Solid colour: confirmed range

PURPLE HAIRSTREAK *Quercusia quercus*

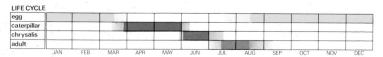

LIFE CYCLE

	JAN	FEB	MAR	APR	MAY	JUN	JUL	AUG	SEP	OCT	NOV	DEC
egg												
caterpillar												
chrysalis												
adult												

Adult identification

Average wingspan 37mm (♀)
to 39mm (♂)

A beautiful butterfly, with inky black upperwings that turn deep purple as they catch the sun. In the male (page 12), this colour is deeper and occurs over all the wings apart from the margins; the purple on females is a large blotch on each forewing, which is visible even in dull light. The underwings are silver-grey with a white streak and a single black-pupilled orange eye beside the tail.

No other butterfly is similar when seen close to. In flight, a White-letter Hairstreak (page 78), Holly Blue (page 98) or Common Blue (page 92) high above the treetops will also reflect the sun, but there is no mistaking the Purple Hairstreak's alternate glint of silver and purple, spinning in the sky above the canopy. On the continent, only the Spanish Purple Hairstreak in the Iberian Peninsula is similar.

Young stages

The **egg** usually occurs singly and is very easy to find at the base of fat flower buds or on twigs on sunny parts of mature Oaks. Look for small grey pin-head sized discs during winter after the leaves have been shed.

On hatching in spring, the **caterpillar** enters bursting Oak buds on which it feeds. Later, it lives inside a silk web spun round the base of a leaf clump, which traps the leaf scales. It emerges at night to browse on leaves. Although perfectly camouflaged by day, the brown, segmented, woodlouse-shaped caterpillar is easy to find in June by feeling the bases of leaf clumps until one feels spongy.

The **chrysalis** can sometimes be found deep inside ant nests among tussocks of grass or under moss at the base of Oaks. It is reddish brown with dark freckles, and produces secretions that attract ants.

Habitat and behaviour

The Purple Hairstreak lives in discrete colonies which fluctuate enormously in size from year to year. A single mature Oak tree of any *Quercus* species can support a colony, but most populations are centred on woods. Although often abundant, the adults are hard to see from the ground, for most of their lives are spent perched on the canopy; tapping the lower boughs often dislodges a few, and occasionally hundreds, of Purple Hairstreaks. However, this butterfly is usually seen in ones or twos, as silver specks tumbling in the

The adult Purple Hairstreak spends most of its life perched, with wings closed, on the top of an Oak tree.

sky above the treetops. Egglaying occurs on bushy growth all over the canopy and down to ground level, with particularly high densities laid on sunny sheltered boughs.

Distribution and status

The Purple Hairstreak is much commoner than is generally realised. It probably occurs in every wood with a reasonable number of oaks throughout Wales and in England south of the Wash. In warm years, the larger oakwoods of these regions support tens or even hundreds of thousands of adults. Smaller numbers will be found in many copses and spinneys, in plantations with occasional oaks, and, less often, on isolated parkland, garden, or hedgerow trees. Further north, the Purple Hairstreak is much more localised, although often overlooked, especially in Scotland.

Numerous colonies have been destroyed where oakwoods have been replaced by conifer plantations, yet small numbers usually persist if nurse trees or cosmetic oaks have been spared. Similarly, it is worth searching any deciduous wood in the south that contains more than one or two oaks.

Colonies of Purple Hairstreak are scarce in Ireland, occurring mainly in hillside oakwoods between Wicklow and Derry, and are common in woods throughout Europe, although naturally absent from the conifer forests of north Scandinavia.

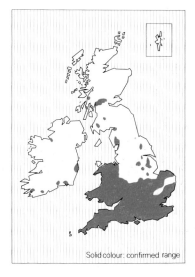

Solid colour: confirmed range

WHITE-LETTER HAIRSTREAK
Strymonidia w-album

LIFE CYCLE

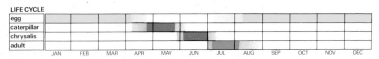

	JAN	FEB	MAR	APR	MAY	JUN	JUL	AUG	SEP	OCT	NOV	DEC
egg												
caterpillar												
chrysalis												
adult												

Adult identification

Average wingspan 36mm
(16mm closed)

This is our darkest Hairstreak. Both sexes look similar, although females tend to have longer tails. The wings are never opened, except to fly, so only the underwings are usually visible. These are blackish-brown, with a thin white line across each wing often, but not always, shaped like a W on its side opposite the tail. There is also a band of orange crescents near the edge of the hindwing.

The rare Black Hairstreak is very similar; see pages 31 and 80 for distinguishing features. In flight, high above a treetop, the White-letter Hairstreak's wings catch the sun and can easily be mistaken for the silver glint of a Purple Hairstreak (page 76). On the continent, it may also be confused with the Sloe, Ilex, False Ilex, and Blue Spot Hairstreaks.

Young stages

One of the easiest ways to find a colony is to search for **eggs** during winter. Look for a single grey disc, shaped like a minute flying saucer, fixed below a flower bud or on a twig on the sunny side of the canopy of a mature Elm.

At first the **caterpillar** enters an Elm flower, on which it feeds, but soon moves to the base of a leaf cluster and thereafter eats leaves. The full grown caterpillar is clear green and lies exposed on the surface of a leaf. It is beautifully camouflaged, but can be spotted quite easily from below in early June by its dark slug-like silhouette.

The **chrysalis** is dark and very hairy, like the Elm twig against which it is often fixed. With practice, it can be found in June.

Habitat and behaviour

Few butterflies are more elusive than this attractive Hairstreak; it is easier to find the young stages than the adult. The caterpillars feed on the flowers and leaves of Elm (*Ulmus* spp.), and may be found on any species, especially Wych Elm. Breeding occurs on trees, not clipped Elm hedges, although a single isolated hedgerow tree will often support a colony; it is worth examining even a young sucker so long as this is large enough to flower. However, the butterfly will more often be found on a tall bushy tree or on a clump of Elms growing in a sunny sheltered position, especially along a wood edge.

Colonies tend to be very small, punctuated by occasional years of abundance. Both males and females spend

This recently emerged White-letter Hairstreak, with its long wing-tails still intact, has made a rare descent from the treetops to feed on flowers.

most of their lives perched high on a treetop, where they bask and drink aphid honeydew. Periodically, an individual will loop high above the canopy in a rapid jerky flight, soon to return to its original bough. Less often one may descend to feed on a flower, where it can be closely approached. In warm still weather, watch also for females flying at all levels over the canopy to lay their eggs.

Distribution and status

Until recently, the White-letter Hairstreak was widely distributed through most of Wales and England, extending well into Yorkshire. Although local everywhere, colonies were much overlooked, and probably occurred in their greatest abundance in the English Midlands and along the Welsh border. Today, most colonies have disappeared, particularly in this region, due to the widespread loss of Elms through Dutch Elm disease.

The current status of this Hairstreak is unknown. Scattered relics are still reported from most regions, but it seems to be surviving best on Wych Elms, especially towards the extremes of its range, for example in Nottinghamshire and further north, and in the West Country. Some colonies have persisted on rejuvenating Elm growth, even

immature suckers, but the outlook for this butterfly is bleak in most areas.

On the continent the White-letter Hairstreak has experienced similar losses, having recently been locally common across the whole of central Europe.

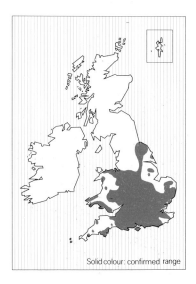

Solid colour: confirmed range

79

BLACK HAIRSTREAK *Strymonidia pruni*

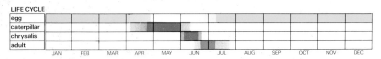

LIFE CYCLE

	JAN	FEB	MAR	APR	MAY	JUN	JUL	AUG	SEP	OCT	NOV	DEC
egg												
caterpillar												
chrysalis												
adult												

Adult identification

Average wingspan 37mm
(16mm closed)

Both sexes of this rarity look much the same and, since the wings are never opened except in flight, only the underwings are visible. These are brown with a golden sheen, and a conspicuous thin white line down each wing, halfway in. The diagnostic feature is an orange border towards the edge of the wings which contains a row of black spots. The tail is quite pronounced. The White-letter Hairstreak (page 78) is often mistaken for this butterfly; note that the white line opposite the tail can be shaped like a sideways on W in both species. The White-letter Hairstreak is the darker butterfly but does not have a row of black spots near the wing edges.

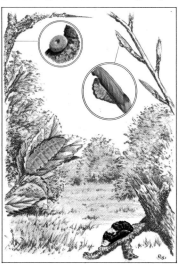

Silhouetted on a treetop, the White-letter Hairstreak looks slightly more triangular, and note, too, the limited geographical range of the Black Hairstreak.

Young stages

The **egg** is an orange-brown flattened disc, covered with minute radiating spikes, and is laid singly at all heights on Blackthorn twigs. It can be found, none too easily, during winter.

The **caterpillar** changes much in its appearance as it grows, from deep chestnut, to chestnut with a white saddle, then becoming greener, and finally translucent green with pale stripes and pink tips to the ridges down its back. It may be found perfectly camouflaged on its food: first on unopened buds, then lying across the bursting scales, and finally exposed in full sunshine among a bunch of fresh leaves.

Marginally the easiest stage to find, the **chrysalis** resembles a bird dropping and is found exposed on top of a Blackthorn leaf or, more usually, on a half shaded twig.

Habitat and behaviour

Typical colonies contain a few adults and are strictly confined to very small areas of a wood or adjoining hedgerow. Any species of *Prunus* can be used for breeding, but Blackthorn (*P. spinosa*) is usual. Tall, sunny, sheltered banks of mature, lichen-encrusted plants are its commonest habitat, although some very large colonies have been supported entirely by young growth. Look for this butterfly, within its range, wherever sunny stands of *Prunus* occur along sheltered wood edges, glades or rides, in tall adjoining hedgerows, or as scrub near woods.

The rare Black Hairstreak often perches on the caterpillar's foodplant, Blackthorn. Despite the name, it is paler and more golden than the White-letter Hairstreak.

The adults seldom fly and almost never stray, preferring to live most of their lives perched out of sight on treetops or tall Blackthorns, where they drink aphid honeydew. It is easy to miss a colony; use binoculars and look, too, for its jerky flight as it seems to hop around the top of a tall bank of Blackthorn. Eventually, an adult will descend to perch or feed on Privet blossom or other flowers, and then it can be approached very closely.

Distribution and status

The Black Hairstreak is a rare butterfly and is confined, with one exception, to the woods of the east Midlands Forest belt, in the basin of heavy clays that lies between Peterborough and Oxford. About 30 colonies remain out of about 60 ever recorded — a good rate of survival compared with most butterflies. Because of their small breeding areas and sedentary behaviour, colonies are usually lost during largescale modern forestry operations; in the past they were similarly vulnerable to the short coppice cycles that were prevalent in much of Britain outside the east Midlands. Today, survival in its traditional woods depends largely on conservation measures, and several fine colonies breed on County Trust Reserves. Elsewhere in Britain, there are probably many places on heavy soils where the Black Hairstreak could

breed nowadays, if it could reach them; for example, one introduced colony in the Weald of Surrey has flourished for 33 years.

In Europe, the Black Hairstreak is found very locally in central regions from northern Spain, across central France, Switzerland and Austria, and more widely in Greece and the Balkans. A few colonies occur in Denmark, Sweden, and Finland.

Solid colour: confirmed range

SMALL COPPER *Lycaena phlaeas*

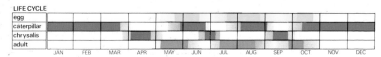

LIFE CYCLE

	JAN	FEB	MAR	APR	MAY	JUN	JUL	AUG	SEP	OCT	NOV	DEC
egg												
caterpillar												
chrysalis												
adult												

Adult identification

Average wingspan 32mm (♂)
to 35mm (♀)

Both sexes of this little butterfly are similar and easy to identify. The upperwings are brilliant: shining copper with black marks and borders on the forewings, and copper borders against a black background on the hindwings. The underwings are equally distinctive: the hindwing is grey-brown whilst the forewing is pale orange with black spots.

Everywhere there is a good deal of variation in the size of the black marks on the upperwings. In central and northern Scotland and in Ireland there is always less black and more clear copper, and Irish underwings tend to be grey. Throughout its range, there is a variety that has a row of blue spots

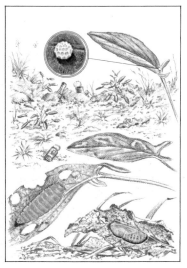

on the upperhindwings; these beautiful specimens are rare in most areas but comprise up to half the adults in parts of northern Scotland.

Nothing in Britain can be confused with this butterfly either in flight or at rest. On the continent there are several other small copper coloured butterflies.

Young stages

Looking like a tiny, white golf ball, the **egg** is very easy to find on small young Sorrel leaves. Look along the midrib, especially near the stem on the uppersurface.

On hatching, the **caterpillar** eats small conspicuous grooves on the underside of a Sorrel leaf. When older, it is slug-like and plain green, often with a pink edge. It rests beneath a leaf, and is quite easy to find at all ages.

The **chrysalis** is very hard to spot in the wild. It is pale brown, flecked with dark specks, and is formed among dead leaf litter.

Habitat and behaviour

This is a conspicuous little butterfly common in rough open places. It lives in more or less discrete colonies which are usually small: larger numbers emerge in the second (August) brood, but even then it is generally seen in ones and twos. After warm summers, a third or even a small fourth brood may emerge in the south, with adults flying late into October. Colonies may be found in open situations on all soils where the foodplants grow. Look especially on ancient grazed grassland, heaths, wasteland, dunes and cliffs, in old pits and quarries, and along sunny woodland rides, embankments, and road verges.

The eggs are laid on Common Sorrel (*Rumex acetosa*) or Sheep's Sorrel

The typical basking posture of a Small Copper with its wings held wide open.

(*R. acetosella*) and very occasionally on Docks. First brood eggs are often laid on quite large, though tender, Sorrel leaves, growing in grass up to one foot tall. In the second brood small plants are greatly preferred, such as develop on unstable or disturbed land, in well-grazed fields, or after a hay crop.

Distribution and status

The Small Copper has declined greatly in many areas, notably in flat regions, due to the intensification of agriculture, the increased shadiness of most woods, the reclamation of heathland, and the lack of sheep or rabbit grazing on unimproved downs. Nevertheless, it is still a common butterfly and may be expected throughout the British Isles wherever its habitats occur. It is absent only from high mountains, parts of northern Scotland, and the outer Scottish Isles.

In Europe, it is also one of the commonest butterflies.

Solid colour: confirmed range

83

SMALL OR LITTLE BLUE *Cupido minimus*

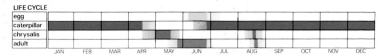

	JAN	FEB	MAR	APR	MAY	JUN	JUL	AUG	SEP	OCT	NOV	DEC
egg												
caterpillar												
chrysalis												
adult												

Adult identification

Wingspan variable: 20mm–30mm, average 24mm

This, our smallest butterfly, is easy to identify. The tiny upperwings have no pattern: females are dark brown, males smokey-black with a dusting of silvery-blue scales near the body. The fringes are clear white with no veining. The underwings are very distinctive: silver-grey with a scattering of tiny black dots (like a miniature Holly Blue, page 98) and none of the orange markings found on other Blues.

Although unmistakable at rest, its silvery wings resemble the two Brown Arguses (pages 88-90) during flight. On the continent, Osiris Blue and Lorquin's Blue are very similar, except that the males' upperwings are clear blue.

Young stages

The **egg** is more easily found than any stage, including the adult. Gently part the 'fingers' of Kidney Vetch flowers in June and look for tiny pale blue discs. There will often be two or three per flowerhead, laid singly by different females.

The young **caterpillar** disappears into a flower (by then a seedcase) to feed on young tissue, but by late July lives openly on the seedhead: look for a pale pinkish-grey grub with its head buried deep into a seed capsule. The full grown caterpillar deserts its plant in high summer to hibernate in a crevice on the ground. Nine months later the **chrysalis** is formed – grey, black spotted and rather hairy – and, like the hibernating caterpillar, almost impossible to find.

Habitat and behaviour

The Small Blue lives in small close-knit colonies in warm sheltered hollows and nooks where the grass is tall enough for Kidney Vetch (*Anthyllis vulneraria*) to flower, yet not so dense that the foodplant ever becomes swamped. Typical sites are the sparse south-facing sides of abandoned chalk and lime pits, embankments, broken cliffs and coombes on downs. Open grassland is very rarely occupied, except in the Cotswolds. Thus the butterfly has a very much more restricted distribution than its foodplant, and even this is not particularly common, being confined to well drained base-rich soils, particularly chalk and lime.

Most colonies consist of a few tens of adults which fly and breed in the same few square yards of ground year after year; emigration occurs only if the habitat has become unsuitable. It is thus easy to miss a colony, especially

The Small Blue usually perches with its wings half open, allowing the sooty upperwings, clear white fringes, and silver underwings to be seen.

since these small dark butterflies are more secretive than Britain's other Blues. The males, especially, prefer to perch for long periods on tussocks or small shrubs. They bask with the wings half open, and fly briefly only to intercept a passing female.

Distribution and status

The Small Blue is widely distributed in Britain, but extremely rare through most of its range. In Scotland, there are one or two inland colonies and perhaps a dozen more along the north and northeast coast. It is even rarer in north England, and in Wales is virtually confined to the southern coastline where, however, it is locally common. There is often a small second brood of adults on southern sites, generally in August. Nearly all surviving English colonies are on the southern chalk and limestone hills, with the Cotswolds being its stronghold; there alone colonies may be expected on most unfertilised hills where there is Kidney Vetch, including open downland. The next best areas are the chalk and limestone hills of

Dorset and the Isle of Wight. In other southern counties it is much more localised, although present in most up to and including the Chilterns.

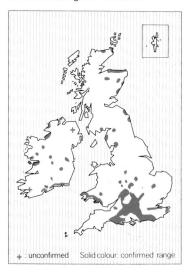

+ : unconfirmed   Solid colour: confirmed range

85

SILVER-STUDDED BLUE *Plebejus argus*

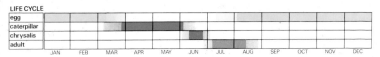

LIFE CYCLE

	JAN	FEB	MAR	APR	MAY	JUN	JUL	AUG	SEP	OCT	NOV	DEC
egg												
caterpillar												
chrysalis												
adult												

Adult identification

Average wingspan 29mm (♀)
to 31mm (♂)

This comparatively small Blue lives mainly on heaths. Distinguishing features of the male's upperwings are the deep blue ground colour and clear white fringes, contrasting sharply with a black border that is much wider than on male Common, Holly or Adonis Blues (pages 32-33). His silver underwings are particularly distinctive; note, on the hindwing the broad band of orange near the edge adjoining black eyespots, each with a bright blue-green pupil. These blue 'studs' are found on no other Blue and give the butterfly its name. On the under forewing, there is no spot nearer to the body than halfway in, in contrast to the spotting on Common, Adonis and Chalkhill Blues.

The female upperwings are dark brown. Although often tinged with blue near the body (especially in northern colonies), she is frequently muddled with the two Brown Arguses (pages 88-91). Examine the underwings, which have the same blue-studded eyes and broad orange band as the male, but on a deep brown background. Her other black spots are unusually large for a Blue, and the pair near the top corner of the hindwing are horizontal (**..**) rather than the colon (**:**) of Brown Arguses.

Young stages

The **egg**, a white disc with minute spikes, is laid singly in midsummer but does not hatch until the following spring. Search for it low down in sparse patches of young Gorse and Heather shoots sprouting from bare ground on heaths. It is more easily found on limestone, inserted into the crack where Bird's-foot Trefoil and other foodplants abut onto bare rock.

The **caterpillar** is well camouflaged and elusive, but sometimes seen as it browses during the day on young leaf-tips (see Habitat for foodplants), always attended by black ants. When full grown, it is green with a dark line down the back, olive and white stripes on the flanks, and shaped like a fleshy wood-louse.

The **chrysalis** is pale brown and buried underground by ants. Occasionally, it may be found inside ant nests under flat stones.

Habitat and behaviour

This is an extremely sedentary butterfly that lives in discrete colonies. Almost all are on heathland, breeding on regenerating growth in recent clearings and burnt areas, or in degenerate

A pair of Silver-studded Blues perch on heather to mate. The male has broad black borders to his blue upperwings, whilst the female's underwings are equally distinctive.

areas where the heather is leggy and light reaches the ground. The butterfly is generally absent from mature heaths, or confined to damp hollows and along rills, where the heather grows sparsely. The caterpillars eat a range of plants, including Heathers (*Calluna vulgaris, Erica* spp.), Gorses (all *Ulex* spp.) and Bird's-foot Trefoil (*Lotus corniculatus*), but always feeding only on tender fresh leafsprouts.

Colonies once bred on a few chalk downs, but all these are now believed extinct. There are, however, certain limestone cliffs where the vegetation grows fairly tall, but very sparsely, among rocks and rubble. The caterpillars feed on Bird's-foot Trefoil, Rockroses (*Helianthemum* spp.) and other low-growing shoots. As on young heathland, some of these colonies are vast, containing tens of thousands of adults.

Distribution and status

This beautiful Blue has become a great rarity in most regions of Britain. Countless colonies have been destroyed or shaded out. Chalk grassland colonies – always rare – were shaded out following the death of rabbit grazers after myxomatosis.

Today, a few populations survive on the heaths of Norfolk, Suffolk, and north Wales, and on dunes along the coasts of Devon, Cornwall and south Wales. The great majority, however, are on the acid heaths of Sussex, Surrey, Hampshire and Dorset. In the New Forest and Dorset it is still locally common, or even abundant, wherever open heathland survives. In addition, large populations occur on limestone on Anglesey and northwest Wales, with smaller numbers in old quarries in Portland, on the Dorset coast.

Solid colour: confirmed range

87

BROWN ARGUS *Aricia agestis*

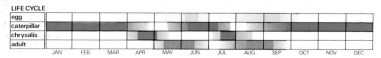

	JAN	FEB	MAR	APR	MAY	JUN	JUL	AUG	SEP	OCT	NOV	DEC
egg												
caterpillar												
chrysalis												
adult												

Adult identification

Average wingspan 29mm

Both sexes of this butterfly look very similar. The upperwings are sooty brown, slightly darker in males, with a black spot in the centre of each forewing and no trace of blue, unlike the female Common Blue. Round the edges is a series of orange crescents which are generally larger on the female. The fringes are white, sometimes just penetated with brown veins. The underwings are superficially similar to those of Silver-studded, Common, Adonis, and Chalkhill Blues, but may be distinguished from the last three by the lack of any spot on the forewing nearer than halfway in to the body, and from all by the spots at the top edge of the hindwing, which form a colon (:). These differences are illustrated on pages

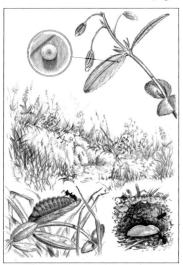

32-33. The Northern Brown Argus (page 90) is generally identical, but has no overlap in range or time of appearance and, in many races, lacks black pupils to the white eyes on the underwings whilst the central spot on the upper forewings is white rather than black. In contrast to the Northern Brown Argus, there are always two generations a year, each, on average, of similar abundance.

Young stages

The **egg** is a pale white disc, laid singly on the undersides of large flat leaves and on the stems of Rockroses, Storksbill or Geranium. It is quite easy to find in late May and again in August in strong colonies.

The **caterpillar** feeds at first on the undersurfaces of the egg plant leaves, making minute perforations from beneath, leaving the clear cuticle intact. These windows are easy to spot, but be warned, some beetles cause similar damage. Second brood caterpillars hibernate when quite small. Later, they feed openly by day on whole leaves, but are beautifully camouflaged being fleshy green with a pink stripe round the edge. They can be found, but not very easily, in April and July by searching for the excited ants which invariably attend them.

The **chrysalis** is pale brown and buried by ants in earth cells, making them very hard to find.

Habitat and behaviour

The Brown Argus lives in small colonies which fluctuate considerably in size. They usually occur on open chalk and limestone grassland, where the caterpillar's main food, Common Rockrose (*Helianthemum chamaecistus*), is

This female Brown Argus is basking on a southern English Down. Many of this butterfly's breeding sites have been lost in recent years due to encroaching agriculture.

abundant. Typical sites are steep south-facing downs, banks or earthworks, where the soil is thin and the vegetation sparse or cropped quite short. Many sites have been destroyed in recent years through agricultural improvement. Colonies also occur on calcareous dunes and cliffs, and, occasionally, in woods, heaths and on heavier soils. On these latter sites, Common Storksbill (*Erodium cicutarium*) and Dove's-foot Cranesbill (*Geranium molle*) are eaten instead.

Whatever the habitat, adults fly freely over open ground, and the males tend to gather at the base of hills and in sheltered hollows, where they await mates. As with most Blues, they often roost communally and can be found at dusk or dawn on sheltered clumps of grass.

Distribution and status

The Brown Argus is a local butterfly that is confined to the southern half of England and to the Welsh Coast. In England, occasional scattered colonies survive in Lincolnshire and on calcareous dunes round the coasts of East Anglia, Devon and Cornwall. The vast majority of colonies are on chalk and limestone downs, notably in the Cotswolds, the Chilterns, the edges of Salisbury Plain, the North Downs escarpment in Kent and Surrey, the South Downs of Sussex, and on the chalk of Dorset and the Isle of Wight. It is still locally common in the extreme south, but very scarce elsewhere. Welsh colonies are much more local-ised, being restricted to calcareous dunes and cliffs along the south and northern coasts and to a very few spots in the west.

Solid colour: confirmed range

NORTHERN BROWN ARGUS
Aricia artaxerxes

LIFE CYCLE

	JAN	FEB	MAR	APR	MAY	JUN	JUL	AUG	SEP	OCT	NOV	DEC
egg												
caterpillar												
chrysalis												
adult												

Adult identification

Average wingspan 29mm

Both sexes of this dusky little butterfly look much the same and almost identical to the Brown Argus. Geography and flight period separate these two species, but they may usually also be distinguished by the presence of a conspicuous white spot in the centre of each upper forewing on the Northern Brown Argus. Note, however that this feature may be absent or reduced in some English colonies. The underwings are also less heavily marked than on the Brown Argus, although the pattern is the same; for example, there is often no black dot in the centre of the white spots.

This butterfly may be distinguished from other blues by the features described for the Brown Argus

(page 88). Note also that its range overlaps only with Small and Common Blues among the 'brown' Blues. The Small Blue has no orange on either sides of the wings and quite different silver undersides; the Common Blue has mainly 'blue' females in these northerly localities.

Young stages

The **egg** is a white disc, similar to that of the Brown Argus but laid on the top rather than beneath Rockrose leaves; consequently it is much easier to find. Look for it from late June in the south, late July in east and north Scotland.

The young **caterpillar** feeds beneath the leaves making small holes with the transparent upper cuticle left intact. When full grown it feeds exposed on Rockrose and is pale green, with short white hairs and a pink stripe that is paler than on the Brown Argus running round the edge. It can be found, but none too easily, tended by ants in late May.

The **chrysalis** is well hidden, being attractive to ants and almost certainly buried in earth cells. It is a pale brownish-green, darker on the wing cases and thorax, with pale pink streaks on the abdomen.

Habitat and behaviour

This dark little butterfly was probably among the first to recolonise Britain after the last ice age. It is now restricted to the chillier parts of the north, although absent from the very coldest areas such as mountains above 350m. It lives in small discrete colonies consisting, usually, of a few hundred individuals at most. These are found on northern limestones and other base rich soils where the caterpillar's food,

90

In Scotland, where this photograph was taken, the Northern Brown Argus has gleaming white marks on the forewings and indistinct spots on the underwings.

Common Rockrose (*Helianthemum chamaecistus*) grows in abundance on south-facing exposures. Typical sites are mountains where there is broken ground or scree, eroding cliffs, or rough open grassland. Rockrose is absent on a few sites and it is believed that the caterpillars eat wild *Geranium* on these; this is certainly an alternative food in captivity.

As with most Blues, the adults roost communally in sheltered pockets at the base of hills, perched head down on grass clumps. In weak sunshine they bask with their wings wide open allowing their dark surfaces to absorb warmth. In brighter sunlight they close their wings and the silvery undersides reflect excessive heat. When warm, they fly frequently and low down over open ground, visiting flowers and searching for Rockroses.

Distribution and status

This is a very local butterfly of Scotland and northern England. The most southerly colonies are a small isolated group in the Peak District of the Pennines west of Sheffield, and there are others in the Lake District and in northeast England, mainly on the Durham coast. Colonies were once much more widespread in these regions, and also in southern Scotland where it is now reduced to scattered sites in the border counties and along the southwest coast of Dumfries, Kirkcudbright, Wigtown and Ayr. It is much more widespread, even locally common, further north in Scotland, especially in north Perthshire, Angus and Aberdeenshire, with a few colonies as far north as southeast Sutherland.

Solid colour: confirmed range

COMMON BLUE *Polyommatus icarus*

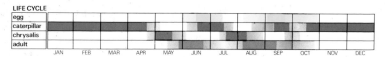

	JAN	FEB	MAR	APR	MAY	JUN	JUL	AUG	SEP	OCT	NOV	DEC
egg												
caterpillar												
chrysalis												
adult												

Adult identification

Average wingspan 35mm (larger in the north)

This is our commonest Blue. Males have unmarked, bright blue upperwings; females orange crescents and dark spots near the outer edges on a ground colour that varies from almost entirely purple-blue to dark brown with a mere tinge of blue near the body. Irish and Scottish females are especially large and blue, and often misidentified as Large Blues. The underwings of both sexes have numerous black spots with white halos, and orange marks round the edges.

The following features, illustrated on pages 32–33, distinguish the Common Blue from similar Blues.

Males

Holly Blues have silver underwings

with tiny black dots.

Silver-studded Blues have broad borders to the upperwings, and blue studs on the underwing.

Adonis Blues are more turquoise (though sometimes similar), with black veins across the white fringes.

Female

Brown Argus and N. Brown Argus have no and Silver-studded Blues little blue on the upperwings and no spot nearer to the body than halfway in on the under forewing. The under hindwings of the first two species have a colon (:) two thirds out from the body near the top edge. The Silver-studded Blue has blue studs.

Adonis and Chalkhill Blues have conspicuous dark veins across the white fringes.

Young stages

The **egg** is a small white disc, laid singly and easily found on the young terminal leaflets of Bird's-foot Trefoil and other foodplants (see Habitat). Search in early July and again in September in the south, and in August in the north.

The plain green **caterpillar** is slightly furry and feeds on its foodplant's leaves by day. It sits exposed on the plant, and although well camouflaged, can be found quite easily when its presence is betrayed by ants, which often attend it for its sugary secretions. Hibernation occurs when quite small, among dead leaves.

The pale green **chrysalis** is formed on the ground and soon buried by ants; it may occasionally be found inside ant nests under stones.

Habitat and behaviour

The caterpillar's usual foodplant is Bird's-foot Trefoil (*Lotus corniculatus*),

The male Common Blue basks with his wings open whenever the sunlight is weak. It lives in discrete colonies but single specimens may wander almost anywhere.

and colonies can be expected anywhere where this grows in reasonable abundance, even in small pockets of land. Typical sites are dunes, cliffs, undercliffs, heaths, wasteland, old quarries, downs and any rough unfertilised grassland that is cropped fairly short. Small colonies are common in overgrown boggy fields and along ditches where Marsh Bird's-foot Trefoil (*L. uliginosus*) is eaten; breeding can also occur on Restharrows (*Ononis* spp.) and Black Medick (*Medicago lupulina*).

The butterfly lives in discrete colonies, although adults occasionally wander and may be encountered anywhere. In the south there are usually two adult broods, and occasionally a third in early autumn. In the north and in Ireland there is a single emergence in July to August. Most populations are small, with one or two hundred adults in summer and even fewer in the first (spring) brood. They flit just above the ground by day and roost communally by night on tall sheltered grass clumps, head down with two to five butterflies per stem. This makes a beautiful spectacle in early morning when they bask before dispersing.

Distribution and status

This is the commonest and most widely distributed of our Blue butterflies. Colonies are found throughout the British Isles and on many of the smaller and most northerly islands, where the females are particularly large, blue and beautiful. It is absent only from the north Shetlands and on mountains above 500m.

Although still ubiquitous along all coasts, numerous inland colonies have been eliminated from flat regions due to the intensification of agriculture. In addition, both the butterfly and its food-plants were shaded out of much rough grassland following the death of rabbits by myxomatosis in the 1950s.

Solid colour: confirmed range

93

CHALKHILL BLUE *Lysandra coridon*

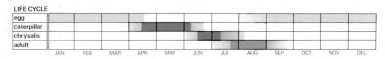

LIFE CYCLE

	JAN	FEB	MAR	APR	MAY	JUN	JUL	AUG	SEP	OCT	NOV	DEC
egg												
caterpillar												
chrysalis												
adult												

Adult identification

Average wingspan 38mm

The large males are unmistakable both in flight and when basking, due to their cold, pale, silvery-blue upperwings. The underwings are also distinctive: heavily spotted on a light grey background that appears almost white in the sun.

The females have chocolate-brown upperwings, tinged to a variable extent by silver-blue near the body. Elderly females overlap with the first Adonis Blues in late August and early September. They differ from female Adonis Blues in having white rather than blue outer circles to the eye spots along the bottom edges of the upper hindwings, and from all other Blues in having brown vein ends across the white fringes, making the edges look chequered.

Young stages

This butterfly hibernates as an **egg**, which is laid singly on the stems of Horseshoe Vetch or tough vegetation near to this plant. It is off white and robust, and easily found from August to October, after which most drop to the ground where they spend the winter. Examine large mats of low growing vetch.

The egg hatches in spring, and as it grows older, the **caterpillar** hides by day below the Vetch but is easily spotted at dusk in early June when it surfaces (smothered by ants which protect it through most of its life in return for sugary secretions) to browse on Horseshoe Vetch leaves. It is very like the yellow striped Adonis Blue caterpillar, which may be on the same plant in April and July.

The pale greenish **chrysalis** also produces sugary secretions and like any stationary sweet object is buried (and protected) by ants in earth cells. Nevertheless it is quite easily found in large colonies.

Habitat and behaviour

As its name implies, this beautiful butterfly is found on flower-rich chalk and limestone grassland, where the caterpillar's foodplant, Horseshoe Vetch (*Hippocrepis comosa*) grows abundantly. Most sites are exposed, south-facing slopes of steep downs or ancient earthworks, and there are many fine colonies in abandoned quarries. Unlike the Adonis Blue, which has the same foodplant, breeding can occur wherever Horseshoe Vetch grows. However the Vetch itself needs fairly short or open conditions, at least for seedling establishment. Many Chalkhill Blue colonies declined and some were lost due to scrubbing up in the years

A mating pair of Chalkhill Blues perch on Round-headed Rampion on a Hampshire Nature Reserve; only the male has milky blue upperwings.

following the death of rabbits by myxomatosis; even more have been destroyed by ploughing and agricultural improvement, which eliminates the Vetch.

The adults fly in compact colonies, although individual males occasionally stray into unlikely habitats. Numbers fluctuate greatly; on the best sites it can be extraordinarily abundant, with tens of thousands of males flitting in a milky blue haze across the open down-land. At night they roost in groups, often at the base of hills, head down and perched two or more to the stem on tall sheltered clumps of grass.

Distribution and status

Colonies are now restricted to the chalk and limestone downs of southern England, but once occurred as far north as Lincolnshire. Today, Cambridge, the Chilterns and Cotswolds mark the northern limit, and it is very local in all these areas, as well as in Avon. Populations have largely been eliminated from the flatter chalklands of East Anglia, Salisbury Plain, and the south, but are still plentiful and to be expected on steep unimproved slopes in the southern counties, especially where the sward is short. Thus a string of colonies breed along the North Downs escarpment of Surrey and Kent, across the Dorset scarps and along the southern Dorset coast, and on the chalk hogsback straddling the Isle of Wight. Other colonies occur commonly on unfertilised south-facing slopes on the South Downs in Sussex, and in Hampshire and Wiltshire. Fortunately many fine colonies are safeguarded by Trust and National Nature Reserves.

Solid colour: confirmed range

ADONIS BLUE *Lysandra bellargus*

LIFE CYCLE

	JAN	FEB	MAR	APR	MAY	JUN	JUL	AUG	SEP	OCT	NOV	DEC
egg												
caterpillar												
chrysalis												
adult												

Adult identification

Average wingspan 38mm

The male has brilliant upperwings of almost turquoise blue, and outer margins edged with a fine black line. The female upperwings are mainly chocolate-brown, but often dusted near the base with turquoise-blue, and have small black eyespots within orange and blue surrounds along the lower margins. Dark veins cross the white fringes in both sexes, just entering the body of the wings. The underwings are spotted with orange near the edges. Many female Adonis and Chalkhill blues are identical, except on the uppersides where the pupil between eyespot and wing edge is blue on this species but white on the Chalkhill blue (page 33). The Common blue has no dark veins across its white fringes in either sex.

Young stages

The **egg** is a white disc with a faint pattern of radiating spikes. It is laid singly beneath the youngest leaflets of Horseshoe Vetch. It is easy to find in June and again in September; examine unshaded plants growing flat against the ground in warm bare depressions, or in pockets of very short turf.

The green and yellow **caterpillar** is beautifully camouflaged as it feeds by day, exposed on tender Horseshoe Vetch leaves. It may be distinguished from the Chalkhill Blue caterpillar by its daytime feeding and the date, and from the Common Blue by its yellow stripes and lack of hairs. It can be found, quite easily, in April and late July by looking for agitated ants which are invariably in attendance 'milking' the caterpillar of sugary secretions. Young second brood caterpillars hibernate on the foodplant in October.

The **chrysalis** is also attended by ants. It is formed underground either inside ant nests or in crevices, where it is soon earthed up by ants in a little cell. It is hard, but not impossible, to find on good sites.

Habitat and behaviour

The Adonis Blue lives in discrete colonies on the very hottest parts of unimproved chalk or limestone grasslands that contain an abundance of the caterpillar's food, Horseshoe Vetch (*Hippocrepis comosa*). Typical sites are steep south-facing downs and ancient earthworks where the sward is so short or sparse that the sun bakes the ground. Other sites are more overgrown, but these support much smaller colonies in which breeding is restricted to a minority of vetch plants, for example along path edges. If sites

A male Adonis Blue sucking moist mud for salts, revealing his brilliant blue upperwings with white fringes that are crossed by short black veins.

cease to be grazed, they soon lose their colony; there was a spate of extinctions after rabbits disappeared from unfarmed downs due to myxomatosis in the 1950s.

Whatever the average size, colonies also fluctuate greatly in numbers from one year to another, and the summer emergence is usually larger than the spring one. Colonies often contain under 100 adults, but after a warm summer, tens of thousands may be seen shimmering above the close-cropped turf of the best sites. Most will be males; the females fly less often and are inconspicuous.

Distribution and status

This is a scarce inhabitant of the warmest downs of southern England. It is locally common on steep downland in Dorset, Wiltshire and the Isle of Wight. Scattered colonies also breed along the escarpment of the North Downs in Surrey and Kent, on some Sussex downs, and, very locally, in Hampshire, Avon and the Chilterns. In the late 1970s it had become reduced to about 75 sites, but with the return of rabbits and sheep to abandoned downs there has been a considerable recovery; perhaps 150 sites supported this

beautiful butterfly in the mid 1980s although it has not recolonised the Cotswolds. The spread of this normally sedentary insect was hastened by the deliberate release of adults· in some regions and by an exceptional build up of numbers on other sites.

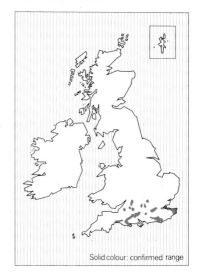

Solid colour: confirmed range

HOLLY BLUE *Celastrina argiolus*

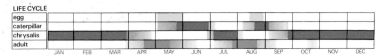

LIFE CYCLE												
egg												
caterpillar												
chrysalis												
adult												
	JAN	FEB	MAR	APR	MAY	JUN	JUL	AUG	SEP	OCT	NOV	DEC

Adult identification

Average wingspan 35mm

Any blue butterfly seen fluttering several feet up around shrubs, trees, along hedgerows or in gardens in southern Britain is likely to be a Holly Blue. This, however, is not a safe means of identification. The most diagnostic feature in both sexes is the underwing, which is clear silver blue with tiny black dots and no orange marks. It gives the Holly Blue a distinctly silver look in flight and makes it unmistakable at rest. Only the Small Blue is similar, but this is very much smaller and has sooty upperwings (page 16). The upperwings of the Holly Blue are violet blue; indeed the male resembles a male Common Blue from above. The female upperwings are more distinctive because they have

wide dark borders and tips, especially in the second brood. However, note that flying females with their inky blue wings can look very like the Large Blue; always check your identification when the butterfly has settled.

Young stages

The **egg** is a white disc that is laid singly and easily found on the flowers or flower buds of shrubs, mainly Holly in springtime and Ivy in the summer brood, although Gorse, Dogwood, Spindle and other bushes may be used.

The **caterpillar** may easily be found among the berries of these plants, lying over a fruit like a green slug, piercing the centre and sucking up the contents, leaving conspicuous feeding damage and droppings everywhere. When full grown, it is pale translucent green, sometimes with purple or rose marks on the flanks and a yellow or white line down the back.

The **chrysalis** is dark brown and formed in a crevice or on the ground, where it is almost impossible to find.

Habitat and behaviour

This attractive little butterfly differs from our other Blues in two important respects. First, it is quite mobile: although more or less resident colonies may persist for many years in certain woods and parks, the adults also roam over wide areas of town and countryside, laying eggs at low densities wherever suitable breeding sites are encountered. The other difference is that it breeds on shrubs rather than low growing vetches and herbs. The fruit of Holly (*Ilex aquifolium*) in spring, Ivy (*Hedera helix*) in summer, as well as Gorse (*Ulex* spp.), Dogwood

A male Holly Blue in his normal perching position with the wings held half open. This Blue may be seen in gardens and parks even in central London.

(*Thelycrania sanguinea*), Spindle (*Euonymus europaeus*) and Alder Buckthorn (*Frangula alnus*) in season. Thus, this butterfly is typically seen in ones or twos, anywhere within its range, in gardens, along hedgerows and, especially, in woods. It often breeds in towns, including central London. Our other blues live in compact colonies in open grassland.

Holly Blue numbers fluctuate greatly from year to year, but are usually highest in the second (August) brood, especially after warm summers. There are two generations of adults in most years, but allegedly just one, in midsummer, in Ireland. In England it is the earliest Blue to emerge, having hibernated as a chrysalis. Search for adults from April onwards, and again in late July and August. It may be seen fluttering high up among shrubs and trees and rarely settles on the ground. It often rests on bushes, usually with the wings closed or no more than half open, so that the silver underwings are always visible.

Distribution and status

The Holly Blue may be seen throughout the southern half of England where Holly, Ivy, and other shrubs flower. In some years it is common over this whole area, and individuals are around suitable shrubs almost anywhere. In other years it is virtually absent for reasons unknown. Despite these fluctuations, there is no reason to believe that it has declined in status in recent years, unlike most butterflies. Elsewhere, it occurs rather locally throughout lowland Wales, in the Lake District, as far north as southwest Scotland, and in Ireland, where it is sparsely distributed throughout.

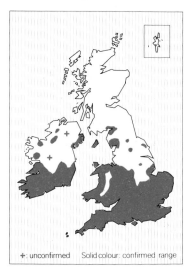

+ : unconfirmed   Solid colour: confirmed range

99

DUKE OF BURGUNDY *Hamearis lucina*

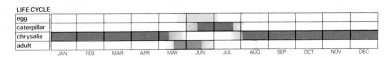

	JAN	FEB	MAR	APR	MAY	JUN	JUL	AUG	SEP	OCT	NOV	DEC
egg												
caterpillar												
chrysalis												
adult												

Adult identification

Average wingspan 29mm (♂) to 32mm (♀)

This little butterfly is the size and shape of a Blue, but has the markings of a Fritillary. The upperwings are blackish brown with pale orange patches in the outer half, and black spots round the edges of all wings. The under forewing is similar, but lighter, whilst the under hindwing has two conspicuous bands of white cells, one third and two thirds out from the body.

All our Fritillaries (pages 36-37), except occasionally the Marsh, are considerably larger, and none has a double band of white on the under hindwing nor spots round every wing edge. In flight it can resemble a very dark Small Copper (page 31) and, even more, the rare Chequered Skipper (page 40). Note

that the latter has a broad head and body, huge eyes, no black spots, and an irregular pattern of white cells on the under hindwing. No other European butterfly is more similar than these.

Young stages

The **egg** is laid in small groups of two to five beneath Cowslip and Primrose leaves. Each is spherical and has a glassy transparent shell through which the creamy contents and, later, the caterpillar's dark hairs are clearly visible. Eggs are easy to find on suitable *Primulas* (see Habitat) early in June but note that fresh eggs resemble those of some moths.

The **caterpillar** is hairy and, when young, can easily be found resting under a *Primula* leaf that has obvious perforations, although again note that moth caterpillars cause similar damage, and so do slugs. When older, it is long, flat, grey-brown, and very hairy, and lives in the leaf litter beneath its plant, emerging to eat leaves at night.

The **chrysalis** hibernates inconspicuously among dead leaves. It is beautifully marked with black spots on a cream background, and has fine hairs.

Habitat and behaviour

The Duke of Burgundy lives in small close-knit colonies in only a few of the places where *Primulas* grow. Typical sites are warm pockets of grassland among scrub on chalk and limestone hills, and sunny sheltered rides, glades, or recent clearings in woodland, where the ground flora is beginning to grow up. In both situations, eggs are laid on large leaved Cowslips (*Primula veris*) or Primroses (*P. vulgaris*) when growing quite prominently in warm spots, sheltered and half-shaded beneath

A typical view of the little Duke of Burgundy, perched with wings half open on a large Cowslip leaf.

shrubs, along ditches, or on the edge of denser woodland. Small exposed *Primulas* growing in open grassland are rejected, as are heavily shaded plants. On many sites this represents a transitional habitat which exists for a few years following a clearing. Within woods, colonies shift as clearings become shaded and new ones are formed. However, colonies seldom move far and, by and large, this is a remarkably sedentary butterfly.

Most colonies are confined to very small areas and contain a few tens of adults, so the butterfly is usually seen in ones and twos. The male is easy to find, for he will perch with wings open on a prominent grass clump or twig, at the edge of a clearing or where woodland rides meet. Any passing butterfly is intercepted in a rapid buzzing flight, female Duke of Burgundys being persued vigorously after which the male will return to his original perch.

Distribution and status

The Duke of Burgundy was once locally common in sunny woods over a large part of southern England, and also bred in Wales and as far north as south Scotland. Few woods are unshaded enough to support a colony any longer, and it is now one of our most rapidly declining species. Perhaps two to three hundred populations survive, but many are small and most are threatened. Fortunately, several fine examples breed on nature reserves.

Despite the decline, scattered colonies can still be found in most English counties south of Gloucestershire and Oxford, but not in Devon or Cornwall. Its probable strongholds, at present, are the scrubby valleys and woods of the Cotswolds. Although extinct in Wales and East Anglia, it survives in three areas further north: around Peterborough, in North Yorkshire, and in the Lake District.

Solid colour: confirmed range

WHITE ADMIRAL *Ladoga camilla*

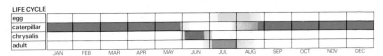

LIFE CYCLE

	JAN	FEB	MAR	APR	MAY	JUN	JUL	AUG	SEP	OCT	NOV	DEC
egg												
caterpillar												
chrysalis												
adult												

Adult identification

Average wingspan 60mm (♂)
to 64mm (♀)

Both sexes of this elegant woodland butterfly look similar, apart from the male's smaller size and slightly darker colour. The upperwings are dusky brown – almost black on young males – with a conspicuous white band across both wings. The underwings have the same pattern, with an extra white area near the body and a lighter, more intricate bronze background adorned with black stripes and spots. Seen close up, no British species looks similar, and the black and white wing pattern is also distinctive in flight. Be warned, however, that hopeful entomologists often mistake an adult silhouetted high in the sky for the Purple Emperor (page 104). The White Admiral is much smaller, with more rounded wings and a daintier flight.

Young stages

The **egg** is laid singly and looks like a miniature sea urchin: round and grey with a honeycomb of ridges over the surface and numerous fine translucent spines. It is quite easy to find on the upper edges of the leaves of suitable Honeysuckles (see Habitat).

In August the spiny brown young **caterpillar** is ridiculously easy to locate, although minute, due to the conspicuous feeding damage. By nibbling the leaf blade back from the tip in a line at right angles to the midrib, it leaves the midrib intact and protruding, and rests on the tip of this. In September it folds the remains of a leaf double with silk cords to hibernate inside. This tent soon withers, but remains and can be found by patient searching during winter, as can the growing caterpillar in spring. When full grown, it is bright green with red-brown spines. Its presence is often betrayed by seeping, nibbled leaves.

The **chrysalis** is as beautiful as the caterpillar. Green and purple with silver points, it has a curious outline including two 'ears' on the head and a prominent knob halfway up. It hangs among Honeysuckle looking like a half-dead, rolled leaf, but can be found with practice.

Habitat and behaviour

The White Admiral is a creature of extensive woodlands. Thin spindly growths of Honeysuckle (*Lonicera periclymenum*) are chosen for breeding: examine wisps dangling in dappled light beneath boughs, and half-shaded plants overhanging ditches or scrambling weakly amongst trees beside a ride.

The White Admiral is a common sight feeding on Bramble in large southern woods.

Vigorous bushy plants with an abundance of flowers sprawling in sunny clearings or over hedgerows are never used. Thus fairly shady woods are the habitat of this butterfly, and it is typical of long abandoned coppices and deciduous forests where the canopy has almost closed. Smaller populations breed along the ride edges of many conifer plantations, but are shaded out as these mature into gloomy plots.

Unlike its young stages, the adult is rather elusive and is generally seen in ones and twos. Long periods are spent basking and drinking aphid honeydew, hidden from view on the forest canopy. It has a swift and elegant flight of short flits and long glides, and soars high into the sky then rapidly down, hugging the contours of the canopy.

Distribution and status

Colonies of White Admiral just penetrate southeast Wales but are otherwise confined to the southern half of England. Its stronghold is the southern central counties of Dorset, Hampshire, Sussex, Surrey, Wiltshire, Berkshire, Buckinghamshire and Oxford, where it is locally common (but seldom abundant) in many small woods, almost all large ones, and can be guaranteed in any large woodland complex, such as those of the West Weald and New Forest. It is much more localised around the fringes of this area, in Somerset, Devon, Avon, the Kent Weald, and in the Midlands as far north as Peterborough. It is scarce in East Anglia and Lincolnshire.

Solid colour: confirmed range

PURPLE EMPEROR *Apatura iris*

LIFE CYCLE

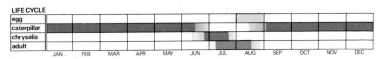

	JAN	FEB	MAR	APR	MAY	JUN	JUL	AUG	SEP	OCT	NOV	DEC
egg												
caterpillar												
chrysalis												
adult												

Adult identification

Average wingspan 75mm (♂)
to 84mm (♀)

Both sexes of this particularly large woodland butterfly look similar, except in sunshine when, at certain angles, the male's upperwings refract the light and turn brilliant iridescent purple. At all other times the ground colour is dusky, with a solid white band across the hindwings and patches of white on the forewings. The underwings have the same white markings as the upperwings, but the ground colour is a beautiful blurred mixture of grey, pink, red-brown and silver, very different from the neat pattern on the White Admiral, the only butterfly with which it can be confused (page 102).

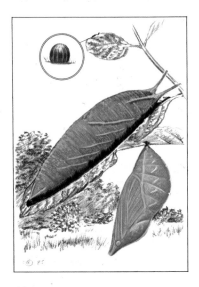

Young stages

The **egg** is as readily found as the adult, although neither is very easy. Search the upper surfaces of suitable Sallow leaves in August. It is dome shaped with fourteen vertical ribs, about 1mm high, and glossy green when fresh but soon developing a conspicuous purple band.

The **caterpillar** is delightfully camouflaged. After the first moult it is 9mm long, grey-brown, with two horns on the head. It hibernates on a silk pad in the fork or crotch of a sallow twig, and can be found by patient searching during winter. The full grown green caterpillar is less often seen. It sits on silk on a Sallow leaf by day, and roams over the bush at night, feeding on leaves before returning to its silk pad.

The **chrysalis** hangs beneath a Sallow leaf where its pale silver-green colour makes it almost impossible to find.

Habitat and behaviour

The Purple Emperor is confined to large forests and to extensively wooded regions where numerous copses and spinneys lie between more substantial woods. It is commonest on heavy soils where the shrub layer contains an abundance of the caterpillar's food-plants: Broad and Narrow Leaved Sallows (*Salix caprea* and *S. cinerea*). Fairly prominent, medium to large sized bushes growing in nooks or beside glades and rides are chosen. The eggs are laid singly on partly shaded leaves within the crown or body of the bush.

This is one of our least conspicuous butterflies. It lives in more or less compact colonies, each colony breeding at low densities over a wide area and usually encompassing several woods. Males congregate on the canopy of a tall tree in one wood,

The male Purple Emperor's wings appear purple like this only when they catch the sun.

usually on a high point, where they perch and make spectacular soaring flights and battle with each other flashing purple as they catch the sun. The same 'master' tree is used year after year, and this is the place to see this beautiful butterfly at its best. Males descend occasionally to drink at puddles or sap, feeding mainly on aphid honeydew on the treetops. The females are seldom seen. After briefly visiting the master tree to mate, they disperse to fly rapidly among shaded branches in search of suitable Sallows, which they enter and promptly disappear.

Distribution and status

Although scarce, the Purple Emperor is often overlooked and is not quite as rare as is popularly supposed. It once bred in most of the heavily wooded districts of Wales and England south of the Humber, but is now largely confined to central southern English counties. Its stronghold is the heavily wooded Wealden Clays of west Surrey and Sussex, where it probably breeds in every copse and wood, extending onto the sandstones and well into Hampshire. There are strong concentrations elsewhere in Hampshire, and very low numbers in the New Forest. Other colonies breed in Wiltshire, and north-east of Oxford. Rare colonies also survive in Dorset, Somerset, Devon, Gloucestershire, Nottinghamshire and East Anglia; not all have been mapped.

Solid colour: confirmed range

105

RED ADMIRAL *Vanessa atalanta*

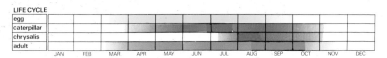

LIFE CYCLE

	JAN	FEB	MAR	APR	MAY	JUN	JUL	AUG	SEP	OCT	NOV	DEC
egg												
caterpillar												
chrysalis												
adult												

Adult identification

Average wingspan 67mm (♂)
to 72mm (♀)

The Red Admiral is one of Britain's largest and most vividly marked butterflies, and is unmistakable whether settled or in flight. The males are slightly smaller but otherwise the sexes look similar. When not flying, it usually basks with its wings wide open, exposing soft velvet black upperwings with a brilliant band of scarlet diagonally across each forewing and round the bottom edge of each hindwing. The top corner of the forewing contains striking white patches, and there is a series of black spots in the lower band of scarlet, with a blue patch at the bottom.

The underside of the forewing is a duller version of the uppersides, and is generally quite conspicuous. However,

when roosting, it is pulled down between the underwings so that only its dark tip is visible. The underwings are then camouflaged to resemble dark bark in shades of mottled brown, grey and black.

Young stages

The **egg** is laid singly on the upper-surface of small young leaves of Stinging Nettles or, occasionally Hop. It is 0.8mm high, and oblong, with eight–ten (usually nine) prominent glassy ridges running from top to bottom. Although pale green at first, it blackens as the embryo develops.

The **caterpillar** feeds on nettle leaves and lives hidden in a tent of one or several leaves, folded over and fastened together by silk. This is quite easy to find in early July and early September. Inside, the caterpillar sits coiled in a 6 shape. When fullgrown (35mm long) it is plump, spiny and very variable in colour; anything from dark, light or olive-brown, with tiny white speckles. There is a broad band of yellow along each side, often broken into patches.

The **chrysalis** hangs suspended inside the caterpillar's last tent. It is pale grey with gold points.

Habitat and behaviour

The Red Admiral may be seen in any habitat and at all altitudes throughout the British Isles, but is commonest around woods, gardens, orchards and hedgerows, where there is both shelter and an abundance of flowers. It is a migratory butterfly that is unable to survive the British winter, except in negligible numbers. Happily, each year adults teem northwards from the Mediterranean, rapidly spreading throughout Europe and always reaching

The magnificent Red Admiral is a regular visitor to gardens throughout the British Isles for much of the summer and autumn.

Britain and Ireland. They are powerful fliers, alternating between strong flits of the wings and glides, and capable of flying well into the night.

The males establish territories along warm edges, such as hedgerows, each patrolling the same areas day after day. After mating, the females search for Nettles (*Urtica* spp.) or rarely Hop, flitting rapidly between plants and generally choosing those that are growing in full sunshine for egglaying; large nettle beds and isolated plants are both used. By late summer feeding becomes a preoccupation, and both sexes are attracted to warm sheltered places containing flowers, such as gardens. They also have a penchant for the juices of rotting fruit and sap from injured trees, and will gather and jostle in orchards and woods where these occur. As the nights get colder, there is some evidence of a return migration to the Continent, but many (probably most) try to hibernate in quite exposed places, and these almost invariably perish.

Distribution and status

Red Admirals arrive in variable numbers from late May onwards and spread throughout the British Isles reaching all our larger islands, including the Shetlands, every year. Even the remotest places such as the central Highlands of Scotland are colonised. Peak numbers are reached one or two broods later, in September when it is usually a frequent, although seldom abundant, butterfly of flowery, sheltered habitats everywhere. In some years it is scarce, but there is no reason to believe that its status is any different than in the past.

Solid colour: confirmed range

PAINTED LADY *Cynthia cardui*

LIFE CYCLE

	JAN	FEB	MAR	APR	MAY	JUN	JUL	AUG	SEP	OCT	NOV	DEC
egg												
caterpillar												
chrysalis												
adult												

Adult identification

Average wingspan 64mm (♂)
to 70mm (♀)

The Painted Lady usually settles with its wings wide open, displaying a chequered pattern of black veins, spots and patches against a background that varies from pale salmon-pink to dull orange. As in the Red Admiral (page 106), there is a small patch of blue on the bottom corner of each hindwing, and the apex of the forewing is black with shining white markings.

The underside of the forewing is a very pale version of its upperside, but the under hindwing is quite different. It has a mottled and intricate pattern of brown, grey, white and blue, with small and slightly fuzzy blue, black and yellow eyespots (page 35).

No other European butterfly is similar

to the Painted Lady. It is the palest and pinkest of all Nymphalids, and appears especially so when flying.

Young stages

The **egg** is laid singly on the uppersides of Thistle leaves and other foodplants, and can be found quite easily in places where the adult has been seen. It is small (0.6mm high), oval, with sixteen prominent glassy ridges running from top to bottom. When laid it is light green, but turns silver-grey as it develops.

The **caterpillar** crawls under its egg-leaf and spins a fine web in which it hides, eating the underside of the (usually Thistle) leaf and leaving distinctive patches of shining outer cuticle that are easy to find. It eventually eats the whole leaf except the spines, and later spins a tent of leaves in which it lives and feeds, becoming increasingly conspicuous as droppings collect in the silk. These tents are easy to find in late June and early July. The caterpillar inside is about 30mm long, black and spiny, with a broken stripe of bright yellow down each side, and a rather square-cut head.

The caterpillar often moves and forms a new tent of thistle leaves where the **chrysalis** develops. This is greyish-pink, delicately burnished with gold, and very beautiful.

Habitat and behaviour

The Painted Lady is a migratory butterfly that may be found, in most years, in any sunny open habitat. It is unable to hibernate and cannot survive the British winter. Our populations originate from N. Africa, where numbers build up each spring leading to annual outbreaks. The adult has a powerful gliding

The Painted Lady is usually seen in open habitats where there is an abundance of flowers for it to feed upon.

flight, and it is one of the great sights of entomology to see them swarming in countless thousands across the Mediterranean and northwards over Europe, eventually settling where the prevailing winds have driven them.

Migrant Painted Ladies occasionally reach Britain in April, and there is a regular, but erratic influx from early June onwards. Individual males soon establish territories on sunny patches of ground a few yards wide in the shelter of hedges, woods and gardens. They bask on the warm earth and periodically make short rapid flights around their beats. When mated, the females seek Thistles (*Cirsium* spp. and *Carduus* spp.) or, less often, Mallows or Nettles for egglaying, flying rapidly between exposed plants, often in cultivated fields. When numbers reach their peak in late summer, adults are seen in all habitats where there are flowers, including gardens, but especially in open warm places such as downs, heaths, dunes, and along the coastline.

Distribution and status

The abundance and range of the Painted Lady varies greatly from one year to the next, depending on the arrival of immigrants and their subsequent success in breeding. In most years they are commonest in the south, but prevailing winds occasionally drive early swarms of immigrants further north, where they breed in large numbers. There is probably no year when a few do not arrive in Britain, and in typical seasons they are encountered, but not necessarily expected, in ones or twos in flowery habitats throughout late summer and autumn. Every few years we have very large influxes, and then the Painted Lady becomes a common sight throughout the British Isles in all habitats up to the Shetlands.

Solid colour: confirmed range

SMALL TORTOISESHELL *Aglais urticae*

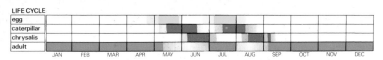

LIFE CYCLE

	JAN	FEB	MAR	APR	MAY	JUN	JUL	AUG	SEP	OCT	NOV	DEC
egg												
caterpillar												
chrysalis												
adult												

Adult identification

Average wingspan 50mm (♂)
to 56mm (♀)

Both sexes of this familiar butterfly look similar. It basks with the wings wide open, displaying bright reddish-orange uppersides with a dark border containing blue crescents around all outer edges. Six black patches break up the orange of each forewing, and there is a white spot near the outer tip. On the upper hindwing, a large area near the body is black, although obscured by orange hairs.

The underwings are sombre and camouflaged to resemble bark. They have a bluish-black inner half followed by a broad indistinct pale band, merging into a blue-black outer margin. The pale area is larger and the pattern more mottled on the under forewing.

No other species in Britain or Europe is likely to be confused with this common butterfly except the extremely rare Large Tortoiseshell (page 35).

Young stages

The **eggs** are laid in large clusters of 80–200, often several layers deep under tender leaves on young Stinging Nettle clumps. Each egg is globular and pale glassy green, with eight or nine prominent ribs running from top to bottom. Batches are easy to find on suitable nettles (see Habitat), but note the similarities with the Peacock (page 114).

Young **caterpillars** live gregariously on white silk webs spun over growths of nettle, splitting into smaller groups of 50–100 as they grow. They are extremely conspicuous, pale at first but becoming darker in later stages. In the final period they live separately, but are still easily found. They reach 22mm long, are spiny, and vary much in colour from yellow with black speckles to mainly black with yellow based spines. See page 114 for the differences of the Peacock. Caterpillars scatter to pupate singly on vegetation or walls, where they are occasionally encountered.

The **chrysalis** varies in colour from lilac-pink washed with copper to dull smoke brown.

Habitat and behaviour

This is a mobile butterfly that does not live in identifiable colonies, but flies freely across the countryside and even out to sea, occasionally reaching France. It may be seen in any habitat, but especially where flowers or Common and Annual 'Stinging' Nettles (*Urtica dioica* and *U. urens*) – the caterpillar's food – are abundant. Depending on the needs of the moment,

The Small Tortoiseshell is one of our commonest butterflies and can often be seen basking on Bramble.

it is commoner in some habitats than in others at certain times of year.

In early spring, adults emerge from hibernation and are mostly seen in sunny situations in the open country-side. The males bask and feed in the morning, then set up territories near nettlebeds in early afternoon, lying in wait for virgin females. Mating occurs deep among nettles and is rarely seen. Then the female leaves to find a suit-able patch for egglaying: young clumps of nettle growing in warm sheltered hollows are preferred, including those in the middle of fields. The next (sum-mer) brood of adults behaves similarly, but their offspring, in August, do little else but feed in preparation for winter hibernation. These gather wherever there are flowers, and are very often attracted to gardens. Hibernation is also often near man's habitations; in garages, lofts, outhouses, cool rooms, and churches. In the north there may be a single emergence each year in July which survives to the following June.

Distribution and status

The Small Tortoiseshell is one of our commonest butterflies and may be expected, in season, wherever there are flowers or nettles anywhere in the British Isles. It is equally numerous on all soil types, reaching the highest mountain tops and our remotest islands, including the Shetlands. However, al-though ubiquitous and common, it is seldom seen in huge numbers at one time, as occurs with our more colonial butterflies.

Small Tortoiseshells are as common and widespread throughout Europe as they are in Britain.

Solid colour: confirmed range

LARGE TORTOISESHELL
Nymphalis polychloros

LIFE CYCLE

	JAN	FEB	MAR	APR	MAY	JUN	JUL	AUG	SEP	OCT	NOV	DEC
egg												
caterpillar												
chrysalis												
adult												

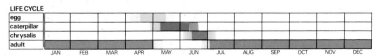

Adult identification

Average wingspan 64mm (♂) to 70mm (♀)

Both sexes of this extremely rare butterfly look similar and, superficially, rather like the Small Tortoiseshell (page 110). Note the duller orange upper-wings of the Large Tortoiseshell, its larger size, the much smaller area of black on the upper hindwing, and that there is an extra black spot but no white patch on the upper forewing. In addition, this species almost never has blue spots along the outer edge of the upper forewing, unlike the Small Tortoiseshell which always does.

The under hindwings look like pale bark, with no sharp pattern. Hairs project from the forewing. In flight, Commas and male Silver-washed Fritillaries are occasionally mistaken for this butterfly.

Young stages

The **eggs** are laid in batches of about 200 forming a sleeve round the slender terminal twigs of tall Elms and other trees (see Habitat). They are inaccessible high up in the Elm canopy and, being pale brown, are hard to see. Each is conical, with seven–nine (usually eight) prominent vertical ridges.

The **caterpillars** live gregariously for their whole lives, resting on conspicuous webs spun over twigs and browsing the leaves beneath them. When full grown, each is velvety black with amber bristles, stripes, white dots and fine hairs, giving a greyish impression overall. It drops to the ground (often from a treetop) to pupate solitarily on a shrub or another tree.

The **chrysalis** is pale brown with gold spots, and looks so like a dead leaf it is very difficult to find.

Habitat and behaviour

The Large Tortoiseshell is a rare butterfly that does not live in stable colonies, but roams the countryside and is generally seen in ones or twos. Despite this, certain wooded districts are – or were – occupied for several successive broods, allowing numbers to build up to local abundance before inexplicably disappearing again for some years. Typical sites are forest edges, avenues, and wooded lanes where clumps of Elm (*Ulmus* spp.) are common. There is little doubt that Elms are the pre-ferred foodplant, although caterpillars have also been found on Sallows, Willows, Aspen, Poplar, Birch, White-thorn, Pear and Cherry.

The adults emerge in high summer to feed briefly before hibernating in hollow trees, wood piles, and sheltered spots. The following March they

The Large Tortoiseshell is unlikely to be seen and may even be extinct as a resident species. It was once an occasional visitor to garden flowers.

re-emerge and can be seen feeding on Pussy Willows or basking with the wings held wide open against warm patches of bare ground. At other times they rarely settle, but fly backwards and forwards among the treetops with a powerful gliding flight that is punctuated by short rapid wingbeats.

Distribution and status

This lovely Nymphalid is our rarest British butterfly and may now even be extinct as a resident species; there are few if any places where one can guarantee or even hope to see it today. One or two genuine sightings are still made each year, but it is hard to know whether these are resident butterflies, vagrants from the continent, or captive stock that has escaped or been released – entomologists regularly return with caterpillars from France where 'nests' are still quite easy to find. Whatever the source, most sightings are made in southern England, with few in Wales, fewer still in Scotland, and none in Ireland.

The last period of comparative abundance for this butterfly was the late 1940s. Periods of extreme scarcity have occurred in the past, but the last 35 years has been an unprecedented time of low numbers, with the more recent loss of many Elms hardly encouraging its recovery.

Possibly now extinct (Records for last 200 years)

Solid colour: confirmed range

PEACOCK *Inachis io*

LIFE CYCLE

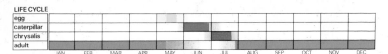

	JAN	FEB	MAR	APR	MAY	JUN	JUL	AUG	SEP	OCT	NOV	DEC
egg												
caterpillar												
chrysalis												
adult												

Adult identification

Average wingspan 63mm (♂)
to 69mm (♀)

This spectacular large butterfly is one of the easiest to identify. The wings have scalloped edges and are often opened, revealing a ground colour of deep chestnut with broad smoky-grey borders. Dominating each hind-wing is the unmistakable 'peacock eye' – glossy blue and black within a fuzzy halo of white. There is also an 'eye' on each forewing, but this is blurred and of mixed colours, as if painted in abstract.

The underwings make a stark contrast, for they are beautifully camouflaged to resemble tree bark. Grey-black, with a steely blue sheen, black wavy lines and prominent black veins, they are darker and less patterned than

the underwings of any related species. An old Peacock seen flying in spring may sometimes be mistaken for the Small Tortoiseshell; note that the latter has a weaker more whirring wingbeat.

Young stages

The **eggs** are laid in batches of up to 500, often six deep beneath tender leaves of Stinging Nettles. Each is pale green and oblong, with eight prominent ridges (looking like fluted glass) running from top to bottom. Batches can be found in early July on the particular nettles used for egglaying (see Habitat). Note that the Small Tortoiseshell's eggs are similar, but are found in May or late July.

The **caterpillars** are gregarious and extremely conspicuous basking on dense webs of silk spun over nettle leaves; nearby leaves are reduced to skeletons. The youngest caterpillars are grey-green, becoming darker at each moult until finally they are velvety black studded with tiny white warts and adorned with shining black forked spines. Over 40mm long, they are larger and much darker than those of the gregarious Small Tortoiseshell, which are also conspicuous on nettles. Full grown Peacock caterpillars scatter to pupate separately in distant vegetation or high up in trees.

The **chrysalis** is yellow-green with pink and gold points.

Habitat and behaviour

Peacock butterflies do not live in strict colonies, but fly freely and powerfully through the countryside, feeding and breeding wherever suitable conditions are encountered. They turn up in most habitats, depending on the season and their activity, but are always commonest in and around woods.

One of our larger more common butterflies is the magnificent Peacock. Here a female basks on Bramble, a favourite nectar source for many butterflies in summer.

On emerging in July, fresh adults are preoccupied with feeding before settling down to winter hibernation. This takes them into gardens and other flowery places, where they are a familiar sight in high summer; woodland rides containing Teasels also attract scores of Peacocks. Hibernation occurs mainly in woods, often inside hollow trees where large numbers sometimes congregate. The following spring, males establish separate territories along wood edges and bushy hedgerows, which the females visit for mating. Egglaying occurs along the same sheltered edges, on large tall clumps of Stinging Nettle (*Urtica dioica*) which catch the sun around midday, when the eggs are laid. Thus, for most of its activities, the Peacock is much more closely connected with woodland than is the Small Tortoiseshell. Although one brood of adults a year is usual, emerging in July and lasting until the following spring, after warm summers there may sometimes be a small second emergence of adults in autumn in the south.

Distribution and status

The Peacock is a common resident throughout most of England, Wales and Ireland, and the large southern populations are reinforced by migrants from the Continent in some years. It becomes much less abundant in the north of Ireland and England, and in the Welsh uplands, where suitable breeding places are few and far between. In Scotland, it may be resident only in the west and only as far north as up to northern Argyll, although migrating individuals may be seen over much wider areas, even occasionally in the Shetlands. There is little reason to believe that the Peacock has declined in status during the present century; indeed, it seems to be spreading in parts of Scotland and Northern Ireland.

Solid colour: confirmed range

115

COMMA *Polygonia c-album*

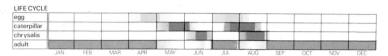

LIFE CYCLE												
egg												
caterpillar												
chrysalis												
adult												
	JAN	FEB	MAR	APR	MAY	JUN	JUL	AUG	SEP	OCT	NOV	DEC

Adult identification

Average wingspan 55mm (♂)
to 60mm (♀)

This is our only butterfly with really jagged edges to its wings. When they are closed, the Comma looks like a dead leaf with a distinctive white comma mark on the hindwing, which gives this butterfly its name (page 23).

The upperwings are orange with brown and black blotches and a dark edge to the ragged outline. In the midsummer emergence, up to one-third of the adults are of a form called *hutchinsoni,* which has faint markings and is brighter and more golden, with less ragged wing edges.

No other British butterfly is remotely similar when seen closeup, although flying adults, and *hutchinsoni* in particular, may be mistaken for Fritillaries.

Young stages

The **egg** is laid singly on the edges of Hop, Nettle, or Elm leaves, and is quite easy to find in sunny pockets along wood edges and hedgerows. It is glassy green and nearly spherical, with ten or eleven prominent white ridges running from top to bottom.

The **caterpillar** lives beneath, and later on top of its leaf, and is as remarkably camouflaged in its own unsavoury way as the adult; it resembles a bird dropping. When small it is dark brown and crusty with white patches, but when full grown it is spiny and tan coloured, with a splash of pure white down most of the back. Once this camouflage is known, the caterpillar is easy to find.

The **chrysalis** is shaped like an upside down sea horse, and is a beautiful pinkish-brown with silver and gold marks. It hangs deep among vegetation and is almost impossible to find.

Habitat and behaviour

The Comma is less migratory than the Peacock and other close relatives, but is fairly mobile and does not live in identifiable colonies. Within a parish it flies between different sites to feed and breed, and is usually seen in ones or twos. Typical habitats are woods, copses, tall hedges, hedged lanes, scrubby corners and mature gardens.

The adults hibernate in woods, and next spring males establish well separated territories, each in a glade or sunny nook along a wood edge, ride or sheltered hedge. He perches on a prominent leaf, leaving to intercept any passing butterfly in a swift gliding flight before returning to the original leaf; passing Comma females are pursued and courted. After mating the females

This female Comma has lighter, less ragged wings than the male.

search for Hop (*Humulus lupulus*), Nettles (*Urtica* spp.) and Elm (*Ulmus* spp.) for egglaying, but choose those plants growing along sunny rides, woodland edges, or sheltered hedges.

Springtime adults look normal, but the first that emerge in midsummer (July/August) are *hutchinsoni*. These behave similarly to the spring Commas and hence are seen mainly around woods. The slightly later emerging midsummer adults are of the normal type and do not breed until next year. Instead they prepare for hibernation by feeding voraciously on flowers, often in gardens. The offspring of the *hutchinsoni* emerge in September, and also look normal and fly to garden, hedgerow and woodland flowers before hibernating.

Distribution and status

The Comma has fluctuated in range and abundance over the past two centuries. In the early 19th century it was locally common and widespread in Wales and England, though scarce in the north. It then declined to become one of Britain's rarest butterflies from the mid 19th century to about 1910. Then a gradual recovery took place but it has yet to reoccupy Yorkshire.

Today the Comma is again a locally common butterfly, to be expected in wooded neighbourhoods throughout all English counties south of a line from Liverpool to the Wash. Occasional sightings may be made further north. It is also locally common in suitable habitats throughout lowland Wales, but is rarely seen at high altitudes.

Solid colour: confirmed range

SMALL PEARL-BORDERED FRITILLARY
Boloria selene

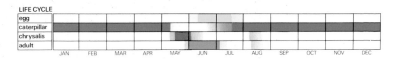

LIFE CYCLE

egg												
caterpillar												
chrysalis												
adult												
	JAN	FEB	MAR	APR	MAY	JUN	JUL	AUG	SEP	OCT	NOV	DEC

Adult identification

Average wingspan 41mm (♂) to 44mm (♀)

Features that distinguish this from other small Fritillaries are illustrated on pages 36-37 and described under the very similar Pearl-bordered Fritillary (page 120). In addition, note that its size is similar to the Pearl-bordered Fritillary, and that their occurence overlaps for at least a fortnight in early June. The upperwings of this butterfly are, on average, brighter and more richly coloured than on the Pearl-bordered Fritillary and the black is darker and glossier. In the west, female Small Pearl-bordered Fritillaries often have distinctive pale marks round the lower hindwings, which shine almost white in the sunshine on old specimens. But it is the underwings that are

diagnostic: bright, variegated, with seven silver 'pearls' round the hind-wing border, six or seven more within the wing, and the rest a contrasting mosaic of pale yellow and red-brown, outlined in black.

Young stages

The **egg** is laid, or dropped, singly among Violets and nearby plants. It is rather tricky but by no means impossible to find; a tiny cone with 18-20 ridges down the sides, that is pale at first, turning grey as it develops.

Hibernation occurs in a curled leaf when the **caterpillar** is half grown. In spring it hides beneath vegetation, surfacing briefly to nibble the lobes of Violet leaves. When found it is unmistakable and very different to the Pearl-bordered Fritillary, due to 12 distinctive rows of amber cones that protude from the dark brown body.

The **chrysalis** is dark brown with silver points and is beautifully camouflaged among the vegetation in which it hangs.

Habitat and behaviour

This and the Pearl-bordered Fritillary share several habitats and still fly together in many places in early June, despite the frightful declines experienced by both. Of these two, this is found in moister, grassier places where Violets are abundant, and seems slightly more tolerant of shading, although it too needs frequent clearings if it is to survive. It is much scarcer on dry soils and, in the eastern half of Britain, is virtually confined to woods. Throughout the wetter west it also breeds in open habitats; search for it on sea cliffs, scrubby valley sides, moist hollows on moors and heaths and in rough sheltered grassland, especially near

The Small Pearl-bordered Fritillary has highly distinctive underwings with a complex pattern of silver, pale yellow and red-brown patches.

the edges of woods. As with related species, Common Dog Violet (*Viola riviniana*) is probably the main food-plant in the south, with Marsh Violet (*V. palustris*) important in the north.

Except in the Highlands, typical colonies are self-contained, breed in small discrete areas, and probably contain one to two hundred adults, although huge numbers may briefly develop in large woodland clearings or on freshly burnt valley sides. In fine weather, the males flit and glide swiftly just above the ground in a restless search for females, pausing only to gorge on nectar from flowers. The females are more secretive, but periodically emerge to flutter over Violets, lay eggs and feed.

Distribution and status

This butterfly is absent from Ireland but is the most widespread and commonest of the smaller Fritillaries elsewhere. It is particularly well distributed on the Scottish mainland (emergence is later in cooler parts of Scotland), being locally common over large parts of the west, although much scarcer in the extreme northwest and southeast, and absent from the Caithness lowlands. Most larger Isles also possess colonies, except for Islay, the Outer Hebrides, Orkneys and Shetlands. Further south colonies are locally common in the English Lake District and through-

out lowland Wales, Devon and Cornwall, especially in woods and along the scrubby coast. Unfortunately, huge declines have occurred almost everywhere else in England. It is now scarce in Dorset, Hampshire, Wiltshire, Surrey and Sussex, and has virtually disappeared from the Midlands and the rest of the east. Shady woods, land drainage, agricultural improvements and the general tidying up of the countryside have all contributed to this decline.

Solid colour: confirmed range

119

PEARL-BORDERED FRITILLARY
Boloria euphrosyne

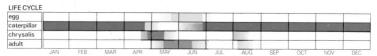

LIFE CYCLE

	JAN	FEB	MAR	APR	MAY	JUN	JUL	AUG	SEP	OCT	NOV	DEC
egg												
caterpillar												
chrysalis												
adult												

Adult identification

Average wingspan 44mm (♂)
to 47mm (♀)

The undersurface of the hindwing is the most distinctive feature of this small springtime Fritillary. The background is a mosaic of orange and yellow, with seven silver 'pearls' along the outer border and another two near the body, one each side of a central orange cell containing a black spot. The Small Pearl-bordered Fritillary (page 36) has the same border, but at least six or seven silver patches towards the body and its background is richer brown, producing a more contrasting pattern. Marsh, Heath and Glanville Fritillaries (page 36) have no silver patches and no central black spot.

The upperwings are bright orange with black veins, crossbars, and black

spots towards the edges (pages 13, 36). They are almost identical to those of the Small Pearl-bordered Fritillary, so the underwings should always be examined. Other small Fritillaries are less golden with heavier black veins, and none has black spots on the upper forewing.

Young stages

The **egg** is laid singly on or near Violets, and is hard to find. Yellow at first, but darkening as the embryo develops, it is conical with twenty to twenty-five fine ridges running from top to bottom.

The **caterpillar** lives solitarily and hibernates among dead vegetation when small. It can sometimes be found in its last stage in late April, basking openly on dead leaves or nibbling Violet leaves. Bright yellow bristles on a black body distinguish this from related caterpillars, although note that the bristles are black on some individuals.

The grey-brown **chrysalis** is usually too well hidden to find, suspended like a dead leaf among dense vegetation.

Habitat and behaviour

This is essentially a woodland Fritillary, although in the west it also inhabits scrubby coastal grassland where gorse is regularly burnt back. Close-knit colonies breed in warm sunny clearings where a flush of young Violets has developed after the clearance of a shady plot. Common Dog Violet (*Viola riviniana*) and Marsh Violet (*V. palustris*) are the main foodplants in the south and north respectively. Typical colonies consist of perhaps a hundred adults confined to a small clearing, but enormous populations can develop, briefly, when an ancient wood is felled and replaced by conifers. These, alas, seldom last long, and are rapidly shaded

A female Pearl-bordered Fritillary laying an egg beside young Violets in a southern English wood. The seven silver 'pearls' that border the hindwing give this Fritillary its name.

out as the plantation matures. In the past, piecemeal coppicing created ideal conditions, allowing this not very mobile butterfly to follow the woodman round his wood, breeding year after year in the new clearings.

The males of this Fritillary are delightful as they flit and glide across woodland clearings and rides, skimming above the ground flora and dipping towards bushes in their search for females. The latter fly less often, but are conspicuous when fluttering round Violets or feeding on the nectar from Bugle and other springtime flowers.

Distribution and status

Until the 1950s this was a common butterfly in English and Welsh woods, at least on dry soils. Since then there has been an extraordinary decline that is still occurring. The main factor responsible is undoubtedly the virtual cessation of coppicing and the increased shadiness of both deciduous and conifer woods, this being one of the first butterflies to be shaded out.

Today, it has largely gone from eastern England, although small relic populations survive in Yorkshire, Kent, Surrey and Sussex. Central counties have fared little better; it is on the verge of extinction in the Midlands, whilst colonies in Oxfordshire, Hampshire, Wiltshire and Dorset are confined to a few tiny clearings within large woodland complexes. Things are better further west. It is still locally common in sunny dry woodland and on some gorsy hills throughout southwest England, lowland Wales, and the Lake District. Scattered colonies also survive, very locally, in woods throughout the Scottish mainland as well as on Rhum and Raasay. Irish colonies are confined to the Burren, where it is quite plentiful.

Solid colour: confirmed range

121

HIGH BROWN FRITILLARY
Argynnis adippe

LIFE CYCLE

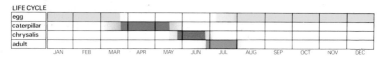

	JAN	FEB	MAR	APR	MAY	JUN	JUL	AUG	SEP	OCT	NOV	DEC
egg												
caterpillar												
chrysalis												
adult												

Adult identification

Average wingspan 60mm (♂)
to 67mm (♀)

High Brown (HB) and Dark Green
(DG) Fritillaries (page 37) look very
similar, with black spots on large golden
upperwings and greenish-orange underwings that differ from the Silver-washed
Fritillary (pages 12, 37) in possessing
large clear-cut silver spots, each outlined in black. HB and DG Fritillaries are
distinguished by the following:

Upperwings
1) Scent cells over the second and
third vein up form elevated, glossy
black streaks in the centre of the male
HB's forewing. These are inconspicuous
on male DGs and absent on females.
2) Female DGs have paler spots round
the outer edges.

Underwings
1) The HB always has a row of small
blurred red eyes with silver pupils on
the hindwing, between the two outer
bands of large silver spots. DGs do not.
2) The DG has obvious silver spots
down the outer edge of the forewing;
the HB has none or, at most, two-three
blurred patches in the corner.
3) The ground colour of the DG's
hindwing is greener, but this varies.

Young stages

The **egg** is a pink cone, turning silver-
grey during winter, with 13-15 ridges
from the base upwards, most of which
reach the top. It is laid singly on dead
vegetation near Violets and is hard to
find (see Habitat).

The solitary **caterpillar** wanders freely
between Violets, often hiding beneath
dead leaves. Full grown, it has twelve
rings of bristles and occurs in two
colour forms: dark brown with a white
stripe and pink bristles, or red-brown
with a white stripe.

The **chrysalis** looks like a dead leaf
and is completely hidden, suspended
among vegetation. Its rather glossy
body is dark brown with gold points.

Habitat and behaviour

The High Brown Fritillary breeds in
sunny sheltered areas containing
scattered shrubs and a warm sparse
ground flora in which violets are abundant. Eggs are laid deep within a bush
or young coppice stool, and the caterpillar basks on the sunny edge or
roams the open ground eating Common
Dog Violet (*Viola riviniana*). Periodic
clearings, fire or grazing are essential
to regenerate the extensive flushes of
violets needed by this species.

Once, colonies were found in clearings

122

The High Brown Fritillary is best identified when it perches with its wings closed. Note the band of small silver dots within red halos towards the outer edge of the hindwing.

in many of the large woods and forests of England and Wales, but most have disappeared during the past 40 years. The majority of modern woods are simply too shady for breeding, and new clearings too isolated from existing sites. In the west, colonies also breed outside woods on neighbouring rough grassland and scrubby hillsides, often flying with the Dark Green Fritillary. These have fared slightly better, and now outnumber the truly woodland colonies.

On all sites, the butterfly lives in fairly compact and sometimes large populations, although single strays may also be found some distance away. The adults fly more among treetops than do smaller Fritillaries, invariably roosting in the higher branches at night and in bad weather. Flight is rapid and soaring, but they also descend to feed avidly on Bramble and Thistle flowers, and can then be closely approached.

Distribution and status

Until the 1950s, the High Brown Fritillary was locally common in large woods throughout Wales and much of England, especially those on well drained soils. Now it is one of our rarest and most rapidly declining species, with losses reported every year. Two colonies survive in Wiltshire, but it is probably extinct in all counties to the east of this as well as in the Midlands, Hampshire, Dorset and Avon. It remains locally common in the Lake District and Malvern Hills, and survives in scattered colonies throughout Wales. Its other 'stronghold' is Devon and Somerset, where small colonies still breed on the fringes of Dartmoor, Exmoor and in a few woods elsewhere.

Solid colour: confirmed range

123

DARK GREEN FRITILLARY
Argynnis aglaja

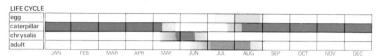

LIFE CYCLE

	JAN	FEB	MAR	APR	MAY	JUN	JUL	AUG	SEP	OCT	NOV	DEC
egg												
caterpillar												
chrysalis												
adult												

Adult identification

Average wingspan 63mm (♂)
to 69mm (♀)

Dark Green and High Brown Fritillaries are often confused, due mainly to the popular yardstick that the former is restricted to rough grassland and the latter to woodland. This simply is not true; both fly together on some sites. Features distinguishing these large Fritillaries are described on page 122 and illustrated on page 37. See also Silver-washed Fritillary, page 126.

Note, on this species, paler spots round the edges of the female's upperwings; no noticeable scent marks on the more golden males; greenish under hindwings (especially in females) that have no red eyes with silver pupils between the outer rows of silver spots; the presence of silver spots on the

under forewing.

The above features are constant, but adults vary in other respects through their range. Irish upperwings are redder-brown; in northwest Scotland and many Western Isles, adults are larger (except on Orkney), much darker and have greener underwings with very large silver patches.

Young stages

The **egg** is conical with 19-22 ridges from the bottom which do not all reach the top. Yellow at first, it develops purple bands and is hard to find on or near bushy clumps of Violets.

The **caterpillar** can sometimes be found basking, moving across the ground, or feeding in sunshine on the lobes, tips and edges of Violet leaves, leaving bite marks. When full grown, the body has a glossy sheen of purple black, with white speckles, red spots along the side, and black bristles.

The **chrysalis** has a dark brown abdomen, black wing cases, head, and thorax, and is completely hidden in a tussock or dense vegetation.

Habitat and behaviour

In general, this spectacular butterfly is found in more exposed places than our other Fritillaries, but note that low numbers sometimes occur in woodland rides and that, nowadays, one is much more likely to see this rather than the very similar High Brown Fritillary in British woods. However, wild open habitats are more usual, typical sites being coastal cliffs, undercliffs, dunes, moorland, flowery downs and unfertilised rough grassland. Depending on the locality, caterpillars eat a range of Violets including Hairy (*Viola hirta*), Marsh (*V. palustris*) and Common Dog (*V. riviniana*). Eggs are laid among large

The male of this mating pair of Dark Green Fritillaries has his wings half open, whilst the female shows the green and silver underwings that are a feature of this species.

isolated bushy clumps or in areas where smaller Violet plants dominate the sward. On most sites, the turf is around 5-15cm tall, kept open by erosion, periodic burning or light grazing.

Adult Dark Green Fritillaries are fast and powerful fliers. They soar up and down hillsides and are approachable only when pausing to feed on Thistles and other flowers. Despite these powers of flight, adults stay within fairly discrete colonies. A few of these consist of vast numbers, but the butterfly is more often seen in ones or twos.

Distribution and status

Although countless populations have been destroyed in recent years by agricultural improvements, this remains our most widely distributed and, in many areas, commonest Fritillary. Its stronghold is the coastline of Ireland, Scotland, Wales and England, except in the east where it is very scarce. With that exception, it is still to be expected, though seldom in any numbers, in all wild coastal habitats round Britain. It is equally well distributed on most islands as far north as Orkney; many beautiful and distinctive races have developed on these isolated sites. Inland, it is locally common in rough hilly areas of

Scotland, Wales and southwest England, but much scarcer in the rest of England, having been eliminated from most flat landscapes. Relic populations survive on unfertilised hills, especially in the Cotswolds, Chilterns and on southern chalk downs.

+ : unconfirmed   Solid colour: confirmed range

125

SILVER-WASHED FRITILLARY
Argynnis paphia

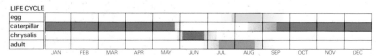

Adult identification

Average wingspan 72mm (♂)
to 76mm (♀)

This is the largest, most magnificent and the latest of our Fritillaries to emerge. The male's upperwings are unmistakable; note the deep orange background, large black spots and lines, and four broad streaks of black scent cells along the central veins of the forewing. The female lacks these streaks, but has larger spots on a duller background, thus creating an impression of a much browner colour both at rest and in flight; no other large Fritillary is so dark. It is the under hindwing (pages 12, 37) that is most distinctive in both sexes: there are four wishy-washy silver streaks down a greenish background, very different from the discrete silver patches of other large Fritillaries.

Some females have a dusky green ground colour on the upperwings and pink on the under forewing. This beautiful form, called *valezina,* is unmistakable when settled or in flight.

Young stages

Each **egg** is laid singly usually three to five feet up a tree trunk that has Violets underneath. It is pale, conical with about 25 vertical ridges, and quite easy to find in late July among chinks in bark on the mossy side of a suitable tree.

The **caterpillar** hibernates before descending to feed in spring. When full grown the body is velvety brown, with darker streaks, twin yellow stripes down the back, and numerous long bristly spines of which two point forward over the head, like horns. Look for it in May and early June, basking on dead leaves or eating the lobes of Violet leaves in sunny pockets within woods.

The **chrysalis** is beautiful but unlikely to be found since it is camouflaged to look like a dead leaf hanging, wet with dew, among dense vegetation.

Habitat and behaviour

This grand Fritillary lives principally in woodland, but also flies and breeds along nearby hedgebanks and lanes in sheltered valleys in Ireland and the West. Slightly darker woods are preferred to those inhabited by other Fritillaries, although colonies are soon shaded out of dense conifer plantations. The best sites are large, recently thinned broadleaved woods, where numerous shafts of light penetrate to the forest floor. The female flutters across the half-lit ground and, on touching Violets, flies up to lay on the nearest tree. Common Dog Violet (*Viola riviniana*) is the main food of the caterpillar.

A male Silver-washed Fritillary (below) and the darker female basking in a Surrey wood.

Silver-washed Fritillaries live in fairly compact colonies, but also stray into neighbouring copses and spinneys that do not support permanent populations. It is a powerful yet elegant flier, preferring sunny glades, rides and edges when not egglaying. Both sexes roost high among tree branches, but swoop down in sunshine to feed on bramble and other flowers or soar up to the canopy to drink aphid honeydew. Courtship is spectacular; the female flies rapidly in a straight line along a woodland ride with the male in hot pursuit looping around her.

Distribution and status

Despite many extinctions, it has fared better than other Fritillaries, perhaps because it can survive in slightly shadier woods. Colonies are commonest in the west, and probably breed in all woods and along many lanes throughout Devon, Somerset, most of Cornwall, west Wales and Ireland. It may be locally abundant in all these regions after a hot summer. It also inhabits most woods slightly further east in Avon, Wiltshire, Dorset, Hampshire and the West Midlands. However, it is much more localised to the east of these, and although locally common in

the West Weald, has almost disappeared from Kent, East Anglia and the East Midlands.

Valezina females are found regularly over a broad area of the central south and may constitute ten percent of females in a warm summer.

valezina
normal range
very rare in north

Solid colour: confirmed range

MARSH FRITILLARY *Eurodryas aurinia*

LIFE CYCLE

	JAN	FEB	MAR	APR	MAY	JUN	JUL	AUG	SEP	OCT	NOV	DEC
egg												
caterpillar												
chrysalis												
adult												

Adult identification

Average wingspan 42mm (♂)
to 48mm (♀); very variable

Although highly variable in both size
and colour, this has, in general, duller,
less distinct, and certainly less golden
markings than Britain's other Fritillaries.
The upperwings are reddish-orange,
with yellow or white patches, and black
veins and crossbars that may be blurred.
It is the only Fritillary to have one row
of black dots around the bottom edge
on both sides of the hindwings but
none on either side of the forewing,
not even on the tip of the underside
(see Glanville Fritillary page 130 and
Duke of Burgundy, page 100). Like the
rare Glanville and Heath Fritillaries, the
underwings have no trace of silver; the
general impression is of dull black and
orange on a dull yellow background.

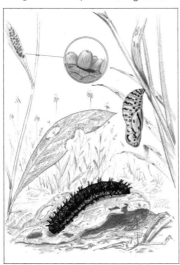

Young stages

Females lay prodigious batches of glossy
yellow **eggs**, heaped up like hard fish
roe on a Devil's Bit Scabious leaf. Each
is oval with about twenty narrow ridges
from the top to halfway down. Egg
clusters soon turn red and can sometimes be found, but the **caterpillars**
are easy to spot. They are bristly and
uniformly black except for tiny white
freckles on the sides, and bask openly
in weak sunlight. In summer they live
gregariously on a web spun over the
foodplant before hibernating in a denser
nest of silk among taller vegetation. In
spring, caterpillars split into small groups
as they grow larger and eventually live
singly, but are still conspicuous.

The **chrysalis** is formed among dense
vegetation and is hard to find. It is
cream with black marks and orange
points.

Habitat and behaviour

The Marsh Fritillary is found in flowery
open grassland where Devil's Bit
Scabious (*Succisa pratensis*) is abundant. Breeding is mainly on medium
sized plants with leaves around 5-15cm
tall, whereas small growths in short
turf and large plants in dense vegetation are both avoided. It lives in two
very different types of habitat: damp
unimproved meadows and boggy hollows
where there is occasional or light grazing,
or dry chalk and limestone downland
that is lightly cropped or abandoned.

The butterfly lives in compact colonies but occasionally strays in warm
years. Numbers fluctuate greatly on
any site from a few tens to many
thousands of adults, depending on the
food supply, weather, and the proportion of caterpillars that were killed
by parasitic wasps. Spectacular out-

A male Marsh Fritillary perches on dead vegetation on an overgrown bog.

breaks occurred regularly in the past, but are rare nowadays, when vast swarms of caterpillars blackened acres of meadowland, eating out the scabiouses before dying in countless numbers through starvation.

Female Marsh Fritillaries usually perch half hidden among tussocks, and may be so laden with eggs that flight is possible only in the warmest weather. The males are more active, and have a curious flitting flight, skimming low over the vegetation as they scan for females.

Distribution and status

This beautiful Fritillary is one of our most rapidly declining species. Most former wetland sites have been destroyed by drainage and agricultural improvements, and the handful of surviving colonies in the eastern half of England and Scotland are on moist heaths or nature reserves. In Wiltshire, Dorset and the Cotswolds it is also close to extinction on boggy farmland, but is actually spreading on chalk and limestone downs, although still extremely local; a few colonies also survive in woodland glades in these counties. Colonies are found more frequently in wet valleys and rough land in southwest England and, especially, in Wales where it is still locally common. Further north, there is still a group of colonies in Cumbria, another in

Inverness-shire, and it occurs on at least eight of the larger Western Isles. The bogs and meadows of Ireland used to be a stronghold, but it has now become extremely localised there, yet still widely distributed, due to reclamation and drainage.

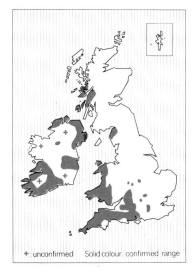

+: unconfirmed   Solid colour: confirmed range

129

GLANVILLE FRITILLARY *Melitaea cinxia*

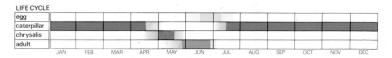

Adult identification

Average wingspan 41mm (♂)
to 47mm (♀)

Both sexes look similar and, like all Fritillaries (pages 36-37), the upperwings have a chequered pattern of black and orange-brown. The dark lines are heavy on this species, and there is a row of black spots in orange circles along the bottom edge of the hindwing. The under hindwing is bright and distinctive, with two bands of orange marks, each outlined in black, on a cream and white background, and more spots near the outer edge. There are also spots on the tip of the under forewing.

The Marsh Fritillary (page 128) has a similar pattern but no spots on the under forewing, it is duller with more orange on the under hindwings. More-

over, the Glanville Fritillary is confined to the Isle of Wight, where, of the smaller Fritillaries, only the Pearl-bordered and Small Pearl-bordered survive. These have silver on the underwings and the upper forewings are more golden with black spots.

Young stages

The **eggs** are laid in batches of 50-200 on Ribwort Plantains (see Habitat). Each is yellow and oval, with around 20 ridges from the top to about halfway down.

The **caterpillars** are extremely conspicuous at all stages. They live gregariously and have black spiny bodies with (when older) shining russet heads that distinguish them from other Fritillaries. When young they bask in hundreds on silk webs spun over Plantains and eat the leaves. In September, an even more conspicuous dense hibernation nest is spun among tall grass, often away from their foodplant. The following spring they grow large and spread out in black swarms over the Plantains. Full grown caterpillars scatter to pupate singly in dense grass and crevices.

The **chrysalis** is purple-grey with black and orange spots, but almost impossible to find.

Habitat and behaviour

This is essentially a central European Fritillary that can just survive in the warmest spots of Britain. It is confined to the south coasts of southern islands, breeding in pockets among crumbling cliffs and undercliffs, and in sheltered south-facing valleys. Search where the terrain is unstable, allowing thousands of Ribwort Plantains (*Plantago lanceolata*) to develop among a sparse sward. The caterpillars eat vast quantities of the

A freshly emerged female Glanville Fritillary resting among Bird's-foot Trefoil on the southern coast of the Isle of Wight.

young Plantain then, rather than starve, switch to tough old growths or to Buckshorn Plantain. Colonies wax and wane rapidly according to the food supply which is dependent on annual slippage and falls along unstable cliffs, for Plantains soon decline where a dense sward develops.

The adults live in more or less compact colonies, although females also stray to lay eggs along cliff tops. Glanville Fritillaries are conspicuous butterflies with a deceptively fast flight of whirring wingbeats punctuated by graceful glides. The males patrol low spots and nooks, sometimes in hundreds, and both sexes can be closely approached when feeding on the nectar from Thrift, Trefoil and other flowers.

Distribution and status

The Glanville Fritillary is one of our rarest butterflies, although it may be numerous where it does occur. Colonies breed around the coasts of most of the Channel Isles and in pockets along much of the southern coastline of the Isle of Wight, especially on sandstone exposures in the western half. There are about twelve more or less permanent colonies on the island, some containing several hundred adults in good years. From these, strays leave

to lay anywhere along the cliff edges and paths, as well as in more conventional habitats.

Odd nests are occasionally found on the chalk downs of the Isle of Wight, and English entomologists often release adults on the mainland. These sometimes establish themselves for a year or two before disappearing.

Solid colour: confirmed range

HEATH FRITILLARY *Mellicta athalia*

LIFE CYCLE

	JAN	FEB	MAR	APR	MAY	JUN	JUL	AUG	SEP	OCT	NOV	DEC
egg												
caterpillar												
chrysalis												
adult												

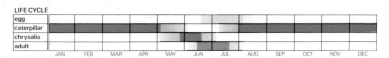

Adult identification

Average wingspan 40mm (♂) to 44mm (♀)

The males of this rare Fritillary are slightly darker and smaller than the females, but otherwise the sexes look similar. The upperwings have the usual Fritillary pattern – a network of dark lines and bars on an orange-brown background – but this is the only species with no brown spots around the edges (pages 36-37). The same absence of both spots and silver patches distinguishes the underwings. These have an elegant pattern of fine veins and orange marks against a cream and white background on the hindwing, whilst the forewing, although usually hidden, is dull orange with a few dark stripes.

Young stages

The **eggs** are laid in large clusters of 50-150, usually under a tough bramble or dead leaf near one of the caterpillar's foodplants (see Habitat). Each is small (0.6mm tall), conical with about 26 vertical ridges, and is pale yellow at first turning grey as the caterpillar develops. Egg batches are well hidden, but the young **caterpillars** can be found on good sites, in groups of ten to twenty on silk spun over their foodplants. They hibernate in similar groups among dead leaves, but live more freely the following spring and bask openly on dead leaves. Full grown caterpillars are easy to find in May, especially on sites with sparse vegetation. They have black heads and bodies, with parallel rows of bristly white and amber cones down their backs.

The **chrysalis** is very pretty but, alas, too well hidden among dead leaves to find. It is white with numerous brown and black markings.

Habitat and behaviour

The Heath Fritillary lives in discrete colonies in exceptionally warm and sunny habitats, sheltered by shrubs or trees, where the caterpillars' foodplants grow in abundance among an otherwise sparse ground flora on poor, well drained or stony soils. Depending on the site, the main plants eaten are Cow-wheat (*Melampyrum pratense*), Ribwort Plantain (*Plantago lanceolata*), and Germander Speedwell (*Veronica chamaedrys*), although other plants, including Foxglove (*Digitalis purpurea*), may be tackled by older caterpillars.

Typical sites are freshly cut woodland (Cow-wheat), recently afforested old grassland (Plantain), and heaths on valley sides on Exmoor (Cow-wheat

A female of the rare Heath Fritillary basking on Bracken in one of its last colonies in Kent. It is one of the four butterflies protected by law in Britain.

again). The habitat is usually ephemeral; the butterfly colonises a clearing, increases at best to thousands of adults after two–four years, then may be entirely shaded out three–seven years later. Unfortunately, colonies are unable to move far, and the lack of a continuous supply of new habitats near to existing sites, as formerly occurred when woods were coppiced, has resulted in numerous extinctions.

Where it survives, the Heath Fritillary is a conspicuous butterfly. Males incessantly patrol woodland rides and clearings, sometimes in hundreds, with a weak gliding flight, pausing only to feed. The females are more secretive, but are also conspicuous on flowers.

Distribution and status

The Heath Fritillary has always been scarce and confined to southern England, but has suffered numerous local extinctions in recent years and is now one of our rarest butterflies. Fortunately, it was saved from the brink of extinction, and today most remaining sites are either nature reserves or managed to maintain suitable conditions.

At present, colonies survive in several compartments of its old famous stronghold, the Blean Forest woods near Canterbury in Kent. Strong populations breed in two woods in east Cornwall, but it is almost extinct in Devon, apart from strong colonies on certain Exmoor hillsides. Several reintroductions have occurred or are planned to refurbish former sites, for example in Essex; early results are promising, but it is too soon to tell if these will survive indefinitely.

The Heath Fritillary is protected under Schedule 1 of the Wildlife and Countryside Act. It is illegal to catch any stage without a licence.

Solid colour: confirmed range

133

SPECKLED WOOD *Pararge aegeria*

LIFE CYCLE

	JAN	FEB	MAR	APR	MAY	JUN	JUL	AUG	SEP	OCT	NOV	DEC
egg												
caterpillar												
chrysalis												
adult												

Adult identification

Average wingspan 47mm (♂)
to 50mm (♀)

This medium-sized Brown often basks with its wings open, revealing an unmistakable pattern of creamy-yellow patches on a deep chocolate background. There are three separate black eyes with white pupils in the patches towards the edge of each hindwing and another eye near the top corner of each forewing. The males have slightly smaller and more blurred yellow markings than the females, and in both sexes the patches are a little paler in the summer brood.

The underwings (pages 12, 38) are beautifully patterned in grey and brown, and resemble a dead leaf when the wings are closed. There are faint marks like mould-spots on the lower wing and

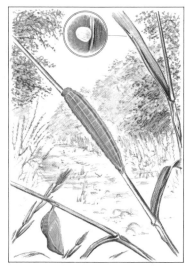

a conspicuous eyespot at the top corner of the forewing. Note its habit of flying in shady places, where its chequered wings perfectly match the dappled light. No other butterfly is likely to be confused with this species.

Young stages

The **egg** is globular with fine striations on the surface and pale yellow with a glassy sheen. Laid singly on grass blades half-shaded beneath shrubs, it is rather difficult to find.

The **caterpillar** is also quite elusive, although it feeds by day on sheltered grasses. It is pale green with faint white and yellow lines, and the 'tails' are white with grey hairs.

The **chrysalis** hangs beneath dense vegetation and is virtually impossible to find. It varies in colour from pale green to dark and even brownish-green. The Speckled Wood can hibernate as either caterpillar or chrysalis, thus leading to a complicated sequence of adult broods.

Habitat and behaviour

The Speckled Wood lives in shadier places than any other native butterfly apart from the White Admiral. Eggs are laid on tender blades of grass growing sparsely in weak light on the woodland floor, or, in more open situations, beneath shrubs. Cocksfoot (*Dactylis glomerata*), Couch (*Agropyron repens*) and probably other grasses are used. Typical sites are dimly lit broad-leaved woods, abandoned coppices, and conifer plantations, although it is shaded out of the latter once the crop matures beyond middle age. The Speckled Wood may also be seen fluttering in dappled light along leafy lanes, tall shady hedgerows (including mature gardens) and among scrub, especially on heavy soils and in damp spots.

This spectacular and unmistakable male Speckled Wood is fond of basking on warm dead leaves, where it is well camouflaged.

The adults feed mainly out of sight, drinking honeydew on treetops, but may descend to jostle with Meadow Browns, Ringlets, and Skippers on bramble blossom in sunny woodland rides. They are usually seen in ones or twos, especially the male which occupies a beam of light in which he perches, basks, and indulges in dancing fluttery flights. He leaves only to ward off other males or to chase females, then returns to his original sunbeam where he can be closely observed for long periods.

Distribution and status

The Speckled Wood became scarce in the 19th century, but has increased its numbers greatly during the past 40 years, no doubt encouraged by the shadier conditions that have been developing in most British woods. Today, it is a common butterfly in almost all woods and copses throughout Ireland, Wales and England south of a line from Liverpool to London. In addition, it is common through the east Midlands Forest belt and there are expanding populations in the Breck and other parts of East Anglia. A few scarce colonies inhabit northern England. As in the south, it is spreading in Scotland and is now locally common in western Argyll, Inverness, up to Inverewe, Ross and on several Western Isles.

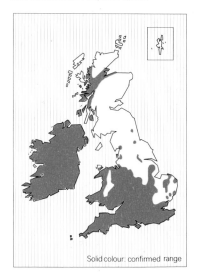

Solid colour: confirmed range

WALL BROWN *Lasiommata megera*

LIFE CYCLE

	JAN	FEB	MAR	APR	MAY	JUN	JUL	AUG	SEP	OCT	NOV	DEC
egg												
caterpillar												
chrysalis												
adult												

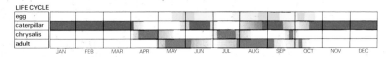

Adult identification

Average wingspan 44mm (♂)
to 46mm (♀)

The Wall Brown (sometimes referred to merely as the Wall) is usually seen basking with its wings open, revealing bright orange upperwings with dark borders, veins and wavy crosslines, and dusky areas near the body. The male (page 16) also has a stripe of dark scent scales diagonally across each forewing. In both sexes there is a conspicuous white-pupilled black eyespot in the top corner of each forewing, and a row of four smaller eyespots around the lower edge of each hindwing.

The underside of the forewing is a paler version of the upperside, but that of the hindwing is very different (pages 16, 38). It is pearl grey with brown zigzag lines across it, and a row of six

eyespots towards the outer edge, each composed of a white-pupilled black spot surrounded by rings of yellow and brown. The bottom spot often has a double pupil. With its wings closed, the Wall Brown blends beautifully with the patches of bare ground on which it usually sits. In flight, its wings are so golden as to be confused with a Comma, or even a Fritillary, but at rest the eyespots and pattern are unmistakable.

Young stages

The **egg** is smooth, almost spherical, and green soon turning to glassy white. It is quite easy to find, singly or in small clusters, on grass roots or fine blades dangling into little sunspots in warm bare recesses and overhangs.

The **caterpillar** feeds at night on grasses in warm pockets or among bare ground, but is fairly difficult to find. It is bluish green when full grown, with faint white stripes.

The **chrysalis** hangs inconspicuously among grass clumps and is unlikely to be found. It varies in colour from pale green to very dark green and even black, with white or yellow spots.

Habitat and behaviour

In contrast to the Speckled Wood, its closest relative, this golden Brown lives in rough open grassland sites where there is plenty of sunbaked ground. The caterpillar can feed on a variety of native coarse grasses, including Tor (*Brachypodium pinnatum*), Wood False Brome (*B. sylvaticum*), Cocksfoot (*Dactylis glomerata*), Yorkshire Fog (*Holcus lanatus*) and Wavyhair Grass (*Deschampsia flexuosa*). Dense swards of grass are ignored, egglaying being confined to occasional plants growing on the edges of bare sunspots, such as hoofprints, rabbit

The Wall Brown usually basks with its wings open on sunny patches of bare ground on rough open grassland where it may be found in small colonies.

scrapes, among rocks, and the crumbling edges of paths. Typical sites are thin-soiled hedgebanks, old quarries, wasteland and disturbed ground, eroding cliffs, and unfertilised downs that are criss-crossed by paths and sheepwalks. It may also be found along road verges and field edges, and also in woods, where egglaying occurs on grass growing sparsely under the sunny sides of shrubs.

Walls live in small discrete colonies. There are normally two broods of adults with the second emergence considerably more numerous than the spring one. After warm summers, there may be a small third brood lasting well into autumn. The adults perch in bare patches of ground, often on paths, basking with their wings two thirds open. When disturbed they fly rapidly for a few yards, then settle further on in another bare patch. The males also patrol areas in search of mates around midday, but switch to perching behaviour in the morning and late afternoon.

Distribution and status

The Wall Brown is a common butterfly of rough ground and unfertilised grassland throughout Wales, except in the mountains, and in most of England. However, it is much scarcer in the far north of England, and absent from high parts of the Pennines. It is common on the Isle of Man, and locally common in much of Ireland, especially in the south. It just penetrates into Scotland, being common around the southwest coast, with rare colonies further north and on a few Western Isles.

Solid colour: confirmed range

137

MOUNTAIN RINGLET *Erebia epiphron*

LIFE CYCLE

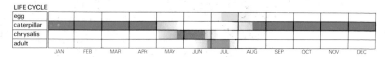

	JAN	FEB	MAR	APR	MAY	JUN	JUL	AUG	SEP	OCT	NOV	DEC
egg												
caterpillar												
chrysalis												
adult												

Adult identification

Average wingspan 35mm (♂)
to 38mm (♀)

This, our second smallest Brown, has slender wings that are deep velvet-brown on the uppersides and very hairy near the body, as indeed is the body itself. Towards the outer edge of each wing is a band of orange blotches, each of which contains a black dot with no white pupil except, very occasionally, on females. Typically, there are four dots on each forewing and three on each hindwing, but this is very variable, as is the sharpness of the blotches. Males tend to be smaller than females and have more blurred markings, but otherwise the sexes look similar. The underwings resemble the upperwings, with less or even no orange blotches and fainter dots.

Only the Scotch Argus is at all similar (page 140), but it is considerably larger than the Mountain Ringlet, with sharper markings and conspicuous black eye-spots containing gleaming white pupils. Note, too, the restricted range of the Mountain Ringlet and that it generally emerges a good month earlier and lives at higher altitudes than the Scotch Argus, although there is some overlap.

On the Continent there are many very similar species of *Erebia*, most of which also live on mountainsides.

Young stages

The **egg** is barrel shaped and quite tall (1mm), with 18-20 ridges running from top to bottom. It is pale yellow with orange blotches, and is laid at the bottom of tussocks of Mat Grass.

The **caterpillar** hibernates when quite small deep in its tussock, and resumes feeding the following spring. When full grown it is green with conspicuous white stripes and twin buff coloured tails. It climbs Mat Grass at night to feed on the tender leaftips. Pupation occurs low down among vegetation.

The **chrysalis** is very pretty: pale green with many neat brown stripes.

Habitat and behaviour

The Mountain Ringlet lives in discrete grassy areas high up on open mountain sides in the Lake District and the Highlands of Scotland. The caterpillars feed solely on Mat Grass (*Nardus stricta*) but the range of this butterfly is very much more restricted than that of its foodplant. Colonies are found at altitudes of 200–1000m, but usually at 500–800m, on damp *Nardus* grassland that is quite tall, yet lightly cropped by sheep or deer. Search for colonies especially along gullies running down the mountain side and in swampy

In fine weather, the male Mountain Ringlet basks for long periods on tussocks of grass. When the weather is dull it sits deep among Mat grass and is very difficult to spot.

hollows bordering streams.

This butterfly flies strictly within self-contained colonies, which may consist of several thousand adults on the best sites. In dull weather they sit deep among the Mat Grass and are easily overlooked. However, when the sun comes out, they suddenly emerge, often in vast numbers, sunning themselves with their wings wide open and fluttering very slowly just above the matted vegetation.

Distribution and status

The Mountain Ringlet has an extremely restricted range in Britain, but where it does occur it is locally common, especially in Scotland. It seems to be maintaining its status very well. Some colonies are large and many live on protected land.

There are two main centres: at high altitudes in the English Lake District and in Scotland, where adults tend to be larger. In Scotland, it lives in the Grampians, from Glen Clova eastwards to Ben Vain and Ben Nevis, and as far north as the hills south of Newtonmore, Inverness. There is also a colony on Ben Lomond. There are unsubstantiated reports from north and southwest Scotland, which have largely been discounted by local experts, and from County Mayo and Lantrim in Ireland.

Irish records date from the nineteenth century, and have been hotly disputed ever since.

+ : unconfirmed   Solid colour: confirmed range

139

SCOTCH ARGUS *Erebia aethiops*

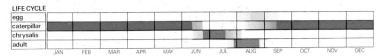

LIFE CYCLE

	JAN	FEB	MAR	APR	MAY	JUN	JUL	AUG	SEP	OCT	NOV	DEC
egg												
caterpillar												
chrysalis												
adult												

Adult identification

Average wingspan 35mm (♂)
to 40mm (♀), smaller in northeast
Scotland

The Scotch Argus has deep velvet-brown upperwings, enlivened by rust coloured spots which are more or less separate on the hindwings but which merge into a bright band across each forewing. Conspicuous white-pupilled black eyespots are set amid the orange, typically three to each forewing and four to each hindwing.

At rest, the forewings are often tucked down, leaving just the under hindwings showing. These are brown with a blurred silver band, very like a dead leaf. The forewing, when protruded, is more conspicuous, with an orange band, a double eyespot near the outer tip, and a single eyespot

further down. Note that the Gatekeeper (page 146) merely has a single black eye containing two white pupils on its under forewing and does not overlap in range.

Male Scotch Argus tend to be smaller, darker and have redder bands than the females, and in northeast Scotland both sexes are smaller than elsewhere, with narrower wings. In southwest Scotland there is often a small fourth eye on the forewing. Only the smaller, rarer and duller Mountain Ringlet (page 138) is anything like similar in Britain.

Young stages

The **egg** is barrel shaped with about 25 ridges running from top to bottom. It is straw coloured with pink freckles and is large, at least 1.3mm tall. It is laid deep in tussocks of Blue or Purple Moor Grass, and although hard to find in the wild, is easily obtained from captive females.

The **caterpillar** hibernates when quite small and is full grown by late June. It is then pale grey-green with green stripes, very like the Gatekeeper caterpillar except that the latter has uniformly white hairs whilst those on the Scotch Argus have brown tips. It may be found at dusk by searching the tender leaftips of Moor Grasses.

The **chrysalis** is pale brown and formed just below the ground in cells of moss in damp places.

Habitat and behaviour

The Scotch Argus lives in rough boggy grassland in Scotland and the Lake District where the caterpillars feed, respectively, on Purple or Blue Moor Grass (*Molinea caerulea* and *Sesleria caerulea*). Colonies are found in wild mountainous regions up to 500m

The Scotch Argus is virtually confined to Scotland in wild mountainous regions up to 500m. The male, shown here, is slightly smaller and darker than the female.

altitude, in places where the food grasses grow quite tall and dense. Typical sites are in warm moist valleys and on rough hillsides, especially along the south and eastern edges of woods or patches of scrub. Smaller numbers may be found inside woods and young plantations, along rides, glades and in recent clearings. Some colonies may also be found on sheltered open moorland.

This butterfly lives in discrete colonies which may consist of over ten thousand adults on the best sites. They are sun loving insects that disappear into the rank grass in poor weather. In sunshine, the males search for mates, flying slowly at grass head height between the tussocks, dipping down to investigate any brown leaflike object. Both sexes may also be found feeding on any available flowers.

Distribution and status

The Scotch Argus is a northern species that was once found in several areas of Cumbria, west Yorkshire, Northumberland and the Durham coast. Most English colonies are now extinct; it is thought that just two populations survive, both in the Lake District.

In Scotland there have also been declines in the southeast, but the larger *caledonia* race remains locally common over large areas of the south-west, at low altitudes throughout the Highlands, and on many Isles of the Inner Hebrides, Arran and others near the west coast. The smaller darker *aethiops* race is also locally common in suitable habitats from east Ross-shire to northeast Perthshire.

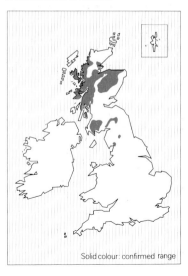

Solid colour: confirmed range

141

MARBLED WHITE *Melanargia galathea*

LIFE CYCLE

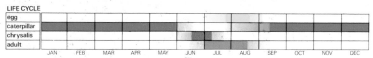

	JAN	FEB	MAR	APR	MAY	JUN	JUL	AUG	SEP	OCT	NOV	DEC
egg												
caterpillar												
chrysalis												
adult												

Adult identification

Average wingspan 53mm (♂)
to 58mm (♀)

This lovely medium sized butterfly has a clear cut pattern of black and white chequered markings on its wings, very different from our other native Browns, and is unlikely to be confused with White butterflies, since they do not have anything like so much black on them. Another difference from the Whites is a series of blue centred black eyespots which are conspicuous, at rest, towards the outer edges of the underwings. The Marbled White's chequered pattern is also recognisable during flight, partly because the wings are flapped very slowly. The ground colour on the underwings varies somewhat from white to pale yellow, and the markings are less distinct, being grey on males and a dusky olive-green

on the females (pages 16, 38).

Young stages

The **eggs** are dropped singly to the ground above patches of tall grass, and are impossible to find in the wild although easily obtained from captive females. They are white and almost spherical, with a slightly granulated surface.

The young **caterpillar** almost immediately hibernates. When full grown the following June it varies in colour from yellow-green to pale brown, with darker green lines down both forms and pink 'tails'. It hides by day at the base of grass clumps but ascends to eat blades at night, and can be found quite easily by torchlight.

The **chrysalis** is hidden in the soil beneath vegetation. It is an anaemic pale brown, and difficult to find.

Habitat and behaviour

The Marbled White lives in tall unimproved grassland and in colonies that have strictly defined boundaries; it will often breed for many years in one field and yet to be inexplicably absent from neighbouring land. This might be due to the species of native grass that are present. Red Fescue (*Festuca rubra*) is thought to be essential in the caterpillar's diet, although Sheep's Fescue (*F. ovina*), Timothy (*Phleum pratense*), Cocksfoot (*Dactylis glomerata*) and Tor Grass (*Brachypodium pinnatum*) may supplement it.

Colonies breed on a wide range of soils, including heavy clays, but are commonest on chalk and limestone. Look for it anywhere within its restricted range where wild grasses grow quite tall, and expect to find it on unfertilised open downland, cliffs and undercliffs. Other typical sites are along woodland rides, road verges and

This marvellous chequerboard of a butterfly is quite different to any other Brown or White. The distinctive pattern is obvious even in flight as the Marbled White flaps its wings very slowly.

embankments.

Many colonies contain merely a few tens of adults, but on lightly grazed or abandoned downs, thousands may be seen flapping lazily above the grass-heads. They alight frequently to feed on Knapweeds, Scabious, Thistles and other tall flowers, or to bask with the wings held wide open whenever the light is weak, for example in late afternoon. In the heat of the day they sit with their wings tightly closed, which reflects rather than absorbs warmth.

Distribution and status

The Marbled White has a curiously restricted range. There is a small group of colonies in the Yorkshire Wolds and others near the south Wales coast. It is common in unimproved fields of the North Downs in Kent but absent from the same downs in much of Surrey. In Sussex it is restricted to the South Downs. Only slightly further west it is a common and ubiquitous butterfly of unfertilised grasslands and woodland rides on most soils throughout central southern and southwest England, except for southwest Cornwall. Colonies were once much more widely distributed in the east Midlands, East Anglia

Lincolnshire and Yorkshire, but nearly all are now extinct. Widespread losses have also occurred within its main range, due largely to agricultural improvements, but happily it remains a common butterfly in southern regions.

Solid colour: confirmed range

GRAYLING *Hipparchia semele*

LIFE CYCLE

	JAN	FEB	MAR	APR	MAY	JUN	JUL	AUG	SEP	OCT	NOV	DEC
egg												
caterpillar												
chrysalis												
adult												

Adult identification

Average wingspan 55mm (♂)
to 60mm (♀); about 32mm closed

This is our largest Brown. The sexes look similar although the female is slightly paler and larger. They always settle with the wings closed, and usually the forewings are tucked out of sight so that only the undersurfaces of the hindwings are generally visible. These are marbled in pale brown and dark and light grey, with no clear cut pattern although there is a zigzag boundary halfway across separating darker markings near the body from a paler outer half. There may be a tiny eyespot near the bottom corner. All in all, it looks like grey bark or dirty sand, and is perfectly camouflaged against the bare spots of ground on which it settles. When the under forewings protrude they reveal a grey border and a brighter,

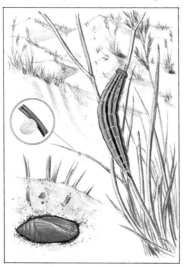

almost orange centre containing two conspicuous black eyespots with white pupils. The upperwings are light brown with bright straw coloured wavy bands and distinctive eyespots, giving the Grayling a richer and brighter appearance in flight than the underwings would suggest, although the overall impression is still of grey. Graylings can be confused with no other species.

Young stages

The **egg** is laid singly on fine grasses or nearby twigs, and can be found by patient searching on good sites. It is white and almost spherical, with 28 fine ridges running from top to bottom.

The **caterpillar** feeds at night on the grass blades and rests deep in the clump by day. Search by torchlight on evenings in early June; it is off white with a greenish-brown head and clear cut yellow, brown and white stripes down its length. It pupates in a small earth cell about 5mm under the ground.

The **chrysalis** is plain reddish-brown and impossible to find in the wild.

Habitat and behaviour

The Grayling occurs in unfertilised grasslands on a wide range of well drained soils, including acid sandstones, shales and chalk hills. It is confined to the most arid places in Britain, where fine grasses grow sparsely among sand, rock or bare earth, and where the sun bakes the ground. Typical sites are heavily grazed downs where chalk or limestone rubble shows through the turf, abandoned quarries, crumbling southfacing cliffs, and, especially, sand dune systems everywhere and southern lowland heaths. It is the characteristic Brown of these two latter habitats. The caterpillars eat a range of native fine grasses,

This Grayling has just alighted on a typical resting place among bare chalk. In a few seconds the forewing, with its conspicuous spot, will be hidden, making the butterfly very hard to see.

depending on local geology, including Bristle Bent (*Agrostis setacea*), Sheep's Fescue (*Festuca ovina*), Marram (*Ammophila arenaria*) and probably Couch (*Agropyron repens*) and others.

Graylings live in discrete colonies, usually containing a few tens or hundreds of adults, although vast populations occur on some heaths and dunes. Most of their lives are spent settled in sunny pockets of bare ground, with the wings tightly closed, leaning edge on to the sun, making them extraordinarily difficult to spot. They cast a shadow only in weak light, when they warm up by sitting sideways to the sun's rays. When disturbed, they fly rapidly in a looping flight for a few yards before floating down into another sunspot.

Distribution and status

Although always a local butterfly, the Grayling was once well distributed in poor arid grassland throughout the British Isles. Recently, most inland colonies have disappeared, due to agricultural improvements, reclamation and changes in land use. They have almost completely disappeared on chalk and limestone downs, where the sward became too coarse and dense in many areas after rabbits disappeared.

Today the Grayling is still locally common on inland heaths in southern Wales and England, notably in Dorset,

Hampshire and the Breck. Otherwise it is largely confined to the coast, where it remains locally abundant and extremely well distributed on rocky cliffs, undercliffs, rough arid grassland, and on dune systems round much of the British Isles. There are, however, large gaps in northeast England and north Scotland. It breeds on most Western Isles, including the Hebrides, but is absent from the Orkneys and Shetland.

+ : unconfirmed   Solid colour: confirmed range

145

GATEKEEPER or HEDGE BROWN
Pyronia tithonus

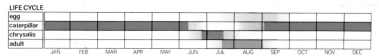

	JAN	FEB	MAR	APR	MAY	JUN	JUL	AUG	SEP	OCT	NOV	DEC
egg												
caterpillar												
chrysalis												
adult												

Adult identification

Average wingspan 40mm (♂)
to 47mm (♀)

This medium sized butterfly looks more golden in flight than any Brown except the Wall Brown (page 136) but is not so bright as to be mistaken for a Fritillary, Comma or the Brown Hairstreak. Seen closeup, it is easy to identify, although beginners sometimes confuse it with the much larger Meadow Brown (page 148). The Gatekeeper's upperwings have broad grey-brown borders enclosing large orange patches, which are especially bright in the males. The males also have a conspicuous dark scent band across the orange on the forewing and are considerably smaller than the females. Both sexes have a large black eyespot usually containing two white pupils near the tip of the forewings, whereas the Meadow Brown's eye has a single pupil, except in Scotland far beyond the Gatekeeper's range. The Gatekeeper also has one, and sometimes several small white dots on the upper hindwing. The undersides are bright mottled brown on the hindwing and dull orange on the forewing, which again bears a diagnostic eye with twin pupils. Note, too, that any dots on the under hindwings are white, whereas those on the Meadow Brown are black.

Young stages

The **egg** is pale with orange blotches, and is laid singly on grass or nearby vegetation sheltered beneath shrubs. It is almost spherical with sixteen or seventeen ridges running from top to bottom, and is very hard to find although it can be obtained readily enough in captivity.

The **caterpillar** hibernates while small, and is easy to find on appropriate grasses in May; search by torchlight at night when they climb to feed on tender grass blades. When full grown it is either fawn coloured or grey with a green tinge, and has dark lines and short white hairs, rather like a Scotch Argus (page 140) or Ringlet (page 154), which, however, has pinker stripes along its flanks.

The **chrysalis** is very hard to find. It hangs below grass or vegetation and is cream with irregular dark streaks and marks.

Habitat and behaviour

The Gatekeeper's other name, Hedge Brown, is more apt, for shrubs are invariably present wherever this little butterfly is found. It is thought that the caterpillars feed on a range of fine and medium leaved wild grasses, including

146

This Gatekeeper or Hedge Brown is voraciously feeding on nectar. Note that the dots on the hindwing are white not black as in the Meadow Brown.

Bents (*Agrostis* spp.), Fescues (*Festuca* spp.), Meadow Grasses (*Poa* spp.) and Couch (*Agropyron repens*), but that they use only medium sized to tallish plants growing in warm spots on the sunny sheltered side of a shrub. The Speckled Wood, in contrast, prefers half-shaded grasses for breeding. Colonies of Gatekeeper can be supported by thin strips of suitable land, and typical sites include hedgerows, warm lanes, rough grassy areas containing scrub and, especially, the edges, rides and glades of sunny woods.

Gatekeepers live in discrete well-defined colonies which, on good sites, consist of thousands of individuals. They have a jerky, fairly rapid flight, and seem to hop in the air moving between flowers, over shrubs and often high among trees. Unlike most Browns, they very rarely fly over open grassland or settle on the ground. They have a penchant for yellow flowers, although Bramble is also a favourite, and are often seen in scores jostling for nectar on Fleabane or Ragwort.

Distribution and status

The Gatekeeper is common wherever wild grasses and shrubs grow together in all southern English counties and throughout lowland Wales. There have certainly been numerous losses in the flatter parts of these regions due to the grubbing up of hedgerows and the general tidying of the countryside, but it is still one of the features of high summer and may be expected in any suitable habitat in the south.

North of the Midlands, it soon becomes a rarity and is increasingly confined to warm scrubby areas near the sea, with the coast of Cumbria being its most northern limit. Similarly, in Ireland it is virtually confined to the southern and southeast coast, although it is often abundant where it occurs.

Solid colour: confirmed range

MEADOW BROWN Maniola jurtina

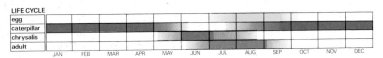

	JAN	FEB	MAR	APR	MAY	JUN	JUL	AUG	SEP	OCT	NOV	DEC
egg												
caterpillar												
chrysalis												
adult												

Adult identification

Average wingspan 50mm (♂) to 55mm (♀); larger in the north

This is the commonest large Brown butterfly in Britain. The male's upperwings are dusky brown with a blurred black patch from the central forewing to the body. In the corner of each forewing is one small white-pupilled black eyespot, usually surrounded by a circle of dull orange. There may also be a faint orange patch below this. This orange patch and the eyespot are both much larger and more prominent on the female. The Meadow Brown often sits with its wings closed, and the lower hindwing may be all that is visible. This is grey-brown with a slight orange sheen and a zigzag boundary that divides a darker inner half from a brighter outer half. There may be one or several small black dots in the outer half. When exposed, the lower forewing is seen as dull orange with a dusky border and a similar eyespot to that on the upperwing.

This butterfly varies somewhat throughout Britain. It is larger and brighter in the North, where the female's eyespots frequently contain two white pupils, like the Gatekeeper. Both sexes become very faded when old. Depending on their age, several Browns look rather like the Meadow Brown in flight, but none should be confused when seen at rest. Note the lack of eyespots on the upper hindwing and see page 39, and accounts of Ringlet (page 154) and Gatekeeper (page 146).

Young stages

The **egg** is laid singly on grass, dead vegetation, or simply dropped to the ground by perched females. It is small (0.5mm tall), almost spherical with 20-24 ribs from top to bottom, and is pale with orange blotches. It is hard to find but easily obtained in captivity.

The **caterpillar** hibernates when small. It is simple to find by torchlight on spring nights when it climbs grass blades to feed. When full grown the body is bright green with a dark green stripe down its back and a pale stripe along each side. The tails are white and the body is covered with white hairs, longer than those on the green caterpillars of other Browns.

The **chrysalis** is green with striking broad black stripes on the wing cases. It hangs beneath a grass stem or vegetation and is hard to find.

Habitat and behaviour

The Meadow Brown may be seen in almost any habitat where wild grasses survive. Several native species are eaten

A female Meadow Brown basking in weak sunlight with her wings wide open. This is the butterfly most commonly seen in the countryside.

by the caterpillar, but those, such as Smooth Meadow Grass (*Poa pratensis*) that have medium sized rather than very fine or coarse blades seem to be preferred. High densities of this butterfly develop in sunny sheltered spots where the sward is left to grow quite tall and lush, whereas it may be absent or in low numbers where the grass is either cropped short or has become dominated by dense tussocks of coarse species. Small strips of suitable grassland will support a colony, and typical sites include road verges, hedgerows and banks, wasteland, cliffs and undercliffs, the edges, glades and rides of sunny woods, and tallish unfertilised grassland, hay meadows and downs everywhere.

The adults fly in distinct colonies which generally have clear cut boundaries and which vary in size from a very few individuals to tens of thousands, depending on the habitat. In weak light, they bask with their wings wide open, but in both dull weather and full sunshine the wings are usually closed. Flight is weak, fluttering, and jerky, just above the grass heads as they move from flower to flower.

Distribution and status

The Meadow Brown is probably the commonest butterfly in the countryside of England, Wales, Ireland and Scotland, but is less often seen in gardens and towns since it seldom flies far from its breeding sites. Although countless colonies have been destroyed by agricultural improvements, especially in lowland Britain, it is still to be expected in any wild grassy habitat, except on northern mountains where it is rarely seen at altitudes above 200m. It is present on most islands, whether large or small, but is absent from the Shetlands. In Orkney, at the limit of its range, it is local and confined to warm south-facing slopes. It is likewise rather local on the north Scottish mainland.

Solid colour: confirmed range

149

SMALL HEATH *Coenonympha pamphilus*

LIFE CYCLE

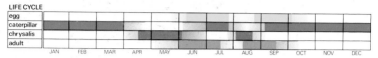

	JAN	FEB	MAR	APR	MAY	JUN	JUL	AUG	SEP	OCT	NOV	DEC
egg												
caterpillar												
chrysalis												
adult												

Adult identification

Average wingspan 34mm (♂) to 38mm (♀); 18mm closed

This is our only small light brown butterfly; female Blues are very much darker, Skippers more golden, and other Browns are considerably larger. The Small Heath always settles with the wings closed, so only the undersides are seen. The under hindwing is pale grey-brown, with slightly darker patches (but no real pattern) near the body, a blurred white mark halfway out, and faint white dots near the outer edge. The forewing is tucked down in bad weather, but usually protrudes as an orange triangle with grey edges and a conspicuous white-pupilled black eye-spot near the top corner. The upper-wings are tawny, making the whole butterfly light brown when flying (pages 16, 38). Only the (much larger) north Scottish race of the Large Heath is similar (page 152).

On the Continent there are many other small species of Heath, but all have distinctive eyespots on the under-hindwing.

Young stages

The **egg** is bowl-shaped with about 50 thin vertical ridges. Pale yellow, with large rust-coloured blotches, it is laid singly and low down on fine grass blades, making it almost impossible to find.

The **caterpillar**, though, is encountered quite often, feeding by day on small grass clumps. When full grown the body is green, with dark white stripes and pink and white pointed tails.

The **chrysalis** is also well camouflaged, but is occasionally found hanging beneath a grass stem; pretty chocolate stripes break up the pale green ground colour.

Habitat and behaviour

The Small Heath is found almost anywhere in Britain where wild fine-leaved grasses survive. The exact range of grasses eaten by the caterpillar is unknown, but Fescues (*Festuca* spp.) and Bents (*Agrostis* spp.) are favourites. Most colonies are rather small, breeding along road verges, hedgerows, sunny woodland rides and in any un-improved grassland. On heavy ground, local dry spots are used, such as boundary banks and ant hills. Better sites occur on well drained soils, especially where the sward is sparse, fairly (but not very) short, and dominated by fine grasses. Often enormous populations develop in extensive areas of this habitat, for example on dunes, heaths, moorland, the coast, and ancient chalk and limstone downs. Elsewhere, it is normally see in ones or twos.

The Small Heath always settles with its wings closed, but is conspicuous only so long as the forewing is held aloft, as it is when the weather is good.

In southern Britain, adults can be seen in variable numbers from mid May to October, as shown in the life cycle chart. The sequence of broods is complicated because some caterpillars develop very much more quickly than others. Further north, there is probably only one emergence of adults each year. This starts in early June in central Scotland, but not until July in the far north.

The adults live in close-knit colonies. Long periods are spent at rest, perched in bare spots and leaning with wings closed towards the sun. Flight, when it occurs, is quite rapid, bobbing and weaving just above the grassheads.

Distribution and status

This is one of the commonest and most widely distributed butterflies throughout Britain, although it is slightly more local in Ireland. Colonies may be found on mountains as high as 750m and on almost all offshore islands, however small, except the Shetlands and Orkney. It remains common on well-drained natural habitats throughout its range, although colonies have been eliminated from most lowland grassland in recent years. Despite this, the butterfly can still be expected in ones or twos along banks and road verges in even the most intensively farmed regions.

Solid colour: confirmed range

LARGE HEATH *Coenonympha tullia*

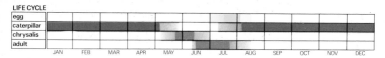

	JAN	FEB	MAR	APR	MAY	JUN	JUL	AUG	SEP	OCT	NOV	DEC
egg												
caterpillar												
chrysalis												
adult												

Adult identification

Average wingspan 41mm; about 22mm closed but larger in N. Scotland

The Large Heath is a grey-brown medium sized butterfly that never basks with its wings open, so only the underwings are clearly seen. The sexes look similar, although the females are often lighter, but there is much individual variation in size, ground colour and spotting within any colony and the predominant type varies greatly in different parts of its range. For simplicity, this variable butterfly is usually classified into one of three forms, although every intermediate exists even, sometimes, in the same population. These are:

1) *davus* (page 38) is the most distinctive and the predominant form in the south. The underwings are dark greenish-grey with a fuzzy zigzag band

running down both wings and a string of eyespots near the outer edge, typically six on the hindwing and two to four on the forewing. These spots are very large, prominent and black, with white pupils and yellow halos.

2) *polydama* is slightly paler and larger than *davus,* with the six eyespots on the hindwing small, rather faint and sometimes lacking white pupils. There are generally one or two similarly reduced eyespots on the forewing.

3) *scotica* (page 38) is the most northerly and largest form, and the opposite extreme in markings to *davus,* being pale, grey and blurred, with few or even no tiny faint eyespots which lack a white pupil.

Despite this considerable variation, no other butterfly resembles the Large Heath, except in its northern *scotica* form which is like the Small Heath but much larger. Note, too, the Large Heath's habitat and short flight period.

In flight, the grey-brown upperwings are revealed, and the whole butterfly appears grey, with little or no trace of the orange.

Young stages

The **egg** is large for the butterfly's size (0.8mm high), almost spherical except for a flattened top, and has about 50 fine ridges running from top to bottom. It is pale, acquiring brown patches as it develops, and is laid singly on the caterpillar's food grasses.

The **caterpillar** hibernates when small. It often feeds by day when it is older, eating grass blades from the tip downwards. When full grown it is 25mm long, grass green with tiny white hairs and pink and white 'tails', and is striped by dark green down the back and white along the sides. No other Brown has so slender a caterpillar

The heavily spotted *davus* form of the Large Heath occurs near the south of its range, as shown here in Shropshire. It is the most distinctive of the three forms.

nor one with so large a head.

The **chrysalis** is bright green with dark stripes on the wing case, much like a large Small Heath's. It is formed hanging beneath any dense vegetation.

Habitat and behaviour

The Large Heath lives in boggy places in the north, where the ground is waterlogged, often submerged, and sometimes treacherous. The caterpillars feed on White-beaked Sedge (*Rhynchospora alba*) Cotton Grass (*Eriophorum angustifolium*) or even Purple Moor Grass (*Molinia caerulea*). Whatever the foodplant, colonies are confined to damp moors, peat mosses, and raised blanket bogs, and may be encountered from sea level up to altitudes of 800m.

Colonies breed in discrete self-contained areas, and may support up to a few thousand adults.

Distribution and status

Colonies of Large Heath may be found throughout Ireland, in central and north Wales, and in the northern half of England, but they are uncommon and local in all these countries. Numerous extinctions have occurred, particularly in England, due to the reclamation of bog.

In Scotland, it was always much commoner and has survived a good deal better. It is widely distributed through most of the lowlands and highlands, but is very much more localised in the south. It becomes progressively more common as one travels further north, and is also found on most Isles, including many that are small and most of the Inner and Outer Hebrides. The northern limit is Orkney.

On the map, boundaries have been drawn where the forms *davus, polydama,* and *scotica* predominate. Note that these divisions are very crude and that many exceptions and intermediates will be found both within colonies and on neighbouring sites.

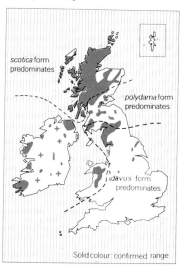

scotica form predominates

polydama form predominates

davus form predominates

Solid colour: confirmed range

153

RINGLET *Aphantopus hyperantus*

LIFE CYCLE

	JAN	FEB	MAR	APR	MAY	JUN	JUL	AUG	SEP	OCT	NOV	DEC
egg												
caterpillar												
chrysalis												
adult												

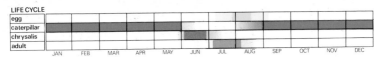

Adult identification

Average wingspan 48mm (♂)
to 52mm (♀)

This medium sized butterfly has dark velvety-brown upperwings that are almost black on the male and only slightly lighter on the female (pages 13, 39). A fine white fringe runs round the outer edges, making a sharp contrast, and there are usually two inconspicuous little black eyespots near the centre of each wing. When settled, the wings are usually closed, revealing the Ringlet's most distinctive feature: a string of conspicuous eyes with white centres surrounded by black then yellow rings. There are generally five to each hindwing with at least two on the forewings, and they gleam conspicuously against a dark, slightly bronzed background.

At rest, the underwings of this butterfly are unmistakable, but old specimens with the wings open look a little like the male Meadow Brown and look very similar when flapping slowly past in flight. Young Ringlets look black when flying.

Young stages

The **eggs** are dropped to the ground among tall wild grasses in damp places, apparently aimlessly by the females. They are impossible to find but can easily be obtained in captivity. Each is globular, slightly conical, with a straw-coloured glassy sheen.

The **caterpillar** feeds on wild grasses, where it also hibernates when quite small. The following spring it rests upright on a stem, falling into the grass clump in a curled ball if disturbed. It is pale brown when full grown with a dark stripe down the back and pale pink and white stripes along the sides. It creeps up to feed on the top grass blades after dusk and can be found quite easily by searching knee high clumps in moist spots by torchlight in early June.

The **chrysalis** is formed within a few strands of silk at the base of a grass clump. It is rounded, pale pinkish-brown with dark streaks and freckles, and is very difficult to find.

Habitat and behaviour

The Ringlet breeds in distinctly damp, but not waterlogged, spots where there are quite tall flushes of native grasses. It is not known exactly which species are eaten by the caterpillars, but the range is certainly small. Tufted Hairgrass (*Deschampsia caespitosa*), Couch (*Agropyron repens*) and Annual Meadow Grass (*Poa pratensis*) are often quoted

The Ringlet is one of the few butterflies that will fly in really overcast weather, and may even be active during light showers.

as favourites. They live in close-knit colonies which may range in size from a handful of adults up to tens of thousands, depending on the site. Numbers also vary from one year to the next, in general being higher after wet seasons.

The largest colonies of this dusky Brown butterfly are found in woodland glades, rides and borders, where the ground vegetation is left to grow tall and lush. Ringlets may occur in moderately shady places, but are rarely found in tall dense conifer plantations. Colonies also breed among scrubby rank grassland and along overgrown hedgerows and verges, especially on heavy soils, but are generally absent from open dry grassland. The adult has a weak fluttering flight and seems almost to hover above the grass heads. It is often seen feeding on brambles, jostling for nectar among Meadow Browns and Skippers.

Distribution and status

The Ringlet is a local but fairly common butterfly in much of England, Wales and Ireland, yet is absent from certain regions such as large parts of northern England and the industrial and urban areas of south Wales, the Midlands and London. Scottish colonies are mainly restricted to the southwest and around Perth and Fife where it is locally common, and there are a few scattered colonies elsewhere, including on some Western Isles. As in the south, it has largely disappeared from industrial southeast Scotland. Many colonies have been destroyed throughout its range by the general tidying up of the countryside, land drainage, and the intensification of agriculture, but it remains one of our commoner butterflies through most of its range.

Solid colour: confirmed range

EXTINCT BUTTERFLIES

In the past 130 years, a number of British butterflies has become extinct: the Large Copper (last colony 1851), Mazarine Blue (1877), Black-veined White (1922) and Large Blue (1979).

The first and last are briefly described because they can, or will probably soon, be seen reintroduced on nature reserves.

LARGE COPPER

Lycaena dispar

Wingspan 40mm (♂) − 42mm (♀)
A beautiful and unmistakable Copper that once lived among the fens of Lincolnshire and Cambridgeshire, breeding along dyke edges and where reeds had been cut. Conspicuous white eggs were laid on the caterpillar's foodplant, Great Water Dock (*Rumex hydrolapathum*). British colonies were of a beautiful subspecies, *dispar,* but this was lost for ever when the fens were drained. In one surviving fragment − Wood Walton Fen, Cambridgeshire, − the habitat has been restored and a similar Dutch subspecies, *batavus,* was introduced in 1927. Numbers fluctuate greatly, and it had to be reintroduced in 1969, but in good years the adults make an unforgettable sight through-

out July. Permission to visit this reserve must be sought from the Nature Conservancy Council.

LARGE BLUE

Maculinea arion

Wingspan 40mm (♂) − 43mm (♀)
The distinguishing features of this magnificent Blue are illustrated on page 32. It once bred on rough hillsides in S. England, notably in the Cotswolds and along the Atlantic coast of Cornwall and Devon. About 30 colonies existed in the 1950s, but soon disappeared, the last surviving until 1979. Most extinctions were caused by undergrazing. The butterfly has an extraordinary life-cycle, feeding first as a caterpillar on Thyme flowers but soon carried underground by a red ant − *Myrmica sabuleti* − to live in its nest for ten months, feeding on ant grubs. Unfortunately, this ant is susceptible to shading, and disappeared along with its caterpillar parasite when sites became overgrown. The habitat can be re-

created, and trials have shown that some continental Large Blues do well in Britain. A reintroduction is planned for the near future if no overlooked native colony is found.

RARE MIGRANTS, VAGRANTS AND ACCIDENTALS

In addition to Britain's three regular immigrants – the Red Admiral, Painted Lady and Clouded Yellow – a few vagrants reach our shores at irregular intervals, and once or twice a century there is a bumper year when several species arrive, some to breed and become locally common. The last time this occurred was in 1945. Unfortunately none of these temporary inhabitants can survive our winters. There is also a growing number of exotic species that escape or are (illegally) released into the British countryside. Our six most regular rare immigrants are described below: those that you can hope to encounter at least once in a lifetime.

BATH WHITE

Pontia daplidice

Although superficially like a female Orange Tip (see page 29) the under hindwings are greener and less fussily patterned, whereas the upperwings have larger, blotchier dark marks. Generally seen in late summer (when rare second brood Orange Tips also fly) on southern cliffs and downs, it is exceedingly rare, but in 1906 and 1945 appreciable numbers arrived and bred on wild Crucifers to produce temporary colonies of tens and even hundreds of adults in a few south coast localities.

CAMBERWELL BEAUTY

Nymphalis antiopa

A gorgeous and unmistakable large Nymphalid with dark chocolate brown upperwings bordered by blue spots and broad cream margins. In contrast to the Monarch, nearly all sightings are in eastern England and Scotland, probably originating from Scandinavia, some perhaps arriving among shipments of timber. It is seen either in late summer or early spring and seems able to withstand our winters as a hibernating adult, but not, apparently, to breed here, even though its foodplants are Willows. Like most migrants, its appearance is sporadic: a few in most years with occasional large influxes, notably in 1846, 1872 and, in this century, 1976 when 272 were reported.

PALE AND BERGER'S CLOUDED YELLOWS *Colias hyale* and *C. australis*

These look almost identical and very similar to *helice* Clouded Yellows (see page 28). None can be distinguished in flight, but *helice* always has broader black edges round the hindwings. The ground colour of all is too variable for identification. Note egglaying plants: Pale Clouded Yellows use Trefoils and Clovers, and have green caterpillars with yellow stripes; Berger's use Horseshoe Vetch and their green caterpillars have yellow and black marks. Note, however, that *helice* lays on all these plants.

Pale and Berger's Clouded Yellows immigrate in most years, and naturalists who frequent southern downs and coasts expect to see one every few years. Berger's is the rarer and *helice* considerably commoner than either. Occasionally large numbers arrive, as in 1900 (2203 reports) and 1945.

MONARCH *Danaus plexippus*

This is by far the largest butterfly to be seen in Britain. Nearly twice the size of a Peacock, its unmistakable orange and black wings span 110mm causing it to flap and glide slowly like a tawny bird. It is an inhabitant of the Canaries and N. America, where there are annual migrations covering thousands of miles. Adults are occasionally blown off course to Britain, but cannot breed here since the Milkweeds that the caterpillars eat are not indigenous. In recent years there have been regular sightings of this highly conspicuous butterfly, mainly in the Scillies, Cornwall, Devon and Dorset notably in 1981 when 140 were reported.

QUEEN OF SPAIN FRITILLARY *Argynnis lathonia*

One or two British sightings are made in most years of this medium-sized Fritillary, which may be distinguished from other Fritillaries by very large and numerous silver patches on the under hindwing which positively glint as the butterfly flies rapidly by. It is generally encountered on open downland in S.E. England in late spring, and, very occasionally, breeds on Violets to produce a short lived brood in August.

Further reading

Ford, E. B. *Butterflies,* Collins, London, 1945. A classic account of butterfly natural history.

Rothschild, M., Farrell, C. *The Butterfly Gardener,* Michael Joseph, 1983. A fascinating account of butterfly farming and gardening.

Oates, M. *Garden Plants for Butterflies,* Masterton, 1985. A must for the butterfly gardener.

Heath, J., Pollard, E., Thomas, J. A. *Atlas of Butterflies in Britain and Ireland,* Viking, Harmondsworth, 1984. A detailed history of the changing status of butterflies.

Brooks, M., Knight, C. *A Complete Guide to British Butterflies,* Jonathan Cape, London, 1982. Beautiful photographs of every stage in all life-cycles.

Whalley, P. *The Mitchell Beazley Pocket Guide to Butterflies,* Mitchell Beazley, London, 1981. The essential pocket field guide to Europe.

Higgins, L. G. and Riley, N. D. *A Field Guide to the Butterflies of Britain and Europe,* Collins, London, 4th edition, 1980. The standard work on European butterflies, but complicated for beginners to use in the field.

Societies to join

British Butterfly Conservation Society (Tudor House, Quorn, nr. Loughborough, Leics., LE12 8AD). Should be joined by everyone interested in the conservation and natural history of butterflies. The BBCS also has regional branches, a junior section, and publishes a splendid bulletin.

The Amateur Entomologists' Society (c/o 355 Hounslow Road, Hanworth, Feltham, Middlesex). An excellent society for amateurs of all ages, especially those with a wider interest in insects. It also publishes a delightful journal.

Local *Nature Conservation Trusts.* There are 46 Trusts covering every county, or group of counties. All are concerned with wildlife conservation and many make a major contribution towards conserving butterflies. Details of your local Trust can be obtained from their national association: *Royal Society for Nature Conservation,* The Green, Nettleham, Lincoln, LN2 2NR. Many Trusts have junior WATCH branches, which provide exciting environmental projects and local activities for all young people up to 18.

Photographic Acknowledgements

Cover: Peacock butterfly, D. W. H. Clark

Margaret Brooks, pages: 56, 91; **D. W. H. Clark,** pages: 26, 45, 47, 49, 51, 53, 55, 57, 63, 71, 73, 75, 77, 81, 83, 89, 95, 101, 107, 109, 111, 113, 115, 125, 143, 147, 149, 155; **Matthew Oates:** 20; **Newnes Books,** page: 5; **J. A. Thomas,** 7, 8, 15, 105, 131; **K. J. Willmott,** pages: 41, 43, 61, 65, 69, 79, 85, 87, 97, 99, 103, 117, 119, 121, 123, 127, 129, 133, 135, 137, 139, 141, 145, 151, 153, 156

INDEX

Page numbers in italic show where illustrations will be found.